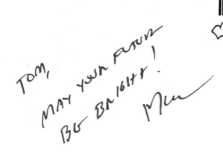

Momentum

HOW COMPANIES DECIDE
WHAT TO DO NEXT

MARC EMMER

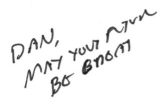

DAN,
MAY YOUR MATH
BE BROAD

ACKNOWLEDGMENTS

WE THANK OUR ADVISORS AND LOYAL CLIENTS INCLUDING:

Ted Allred, Dana Borowka, Chris Braun, Gary Brennglass, Richard Brent, Scott Capistrano, Larry Comp, Jed Daly, Rick Dawson, Gary Fish, David Fisher, Jon Georgio, Ron Georgio, Dan Goetz, Bill Hawfield, Jessica Hawthorne-Castro, Jeffrey Knakal, Dan Kravitz, Michael LaLonde, Mitzi Like, Robert McCarthy, Mitch Pearlman, Trevor Rice, Gail Schaper-Gordon, John Shaffery, Dewayne Sode, Dale Van Dellen, John Vance, and Casey Xiao-Morris.

In memory of Steve Saperstein and Lloyd Sreden.

To my family: Kerri, Megan and Brooke, you give my life meaning.

CONTENTS

Part 1

GAINING MOMENTUM

FOREWORD:
WHY STRATEGY?

"Fortune favors the well-prepared."
—Dr. Louis Pasteur

THE PRESIDENTIAL MEDAL OF FREEDOM is the highest honor that can be bestowed on an American citizen. In November 2016, legendary Los Angeles Dodgers announcer Vin Scully was honored with the award at a star-studded event in the East Room of the White House.

Scully called Hank Aaron's 715th home run, Don Larsen's perfect game and Dodgers broadcasts for sixty-seven years. Scully's commentary was informative, witty and packed with legendary stories.

At the presentation of his award by President Obama, Scully stood teary-eyed, seemingly embarrassed by all the attention. He shared a stage with Michael Jordan, Bill Gates, Diana Ross and 18 other beacons of American culture.

After the ceremony, Scully was interviewed by John Dickerson on *Face the Nation*. Dickerson asked him about his keys to success as a broadcaster. Scully quoted Laurence Olivier, who said, "My success comes from a humility to prepare and a confidence to bring it off."

I found Scully's comment stunning but only mildly surprising. Scully was acknowledging that his mastery as a broadcaster had less to do with what he did in the booth, and more to do with what he did before he climbed into it. His sixty-seven years of experience did not provide him ample background to wing it.

I have had the honor to work with some extraordinary people—wildly successful entrepreneurs. The common thread among them is that they possess the humility to prepare. Part of their preparation has been their willingness to gather feedback from customers, employees, board members and advisors like me. It seems the most successful of people are the ones who know they don't have it all figured out. They are the ones who listen before they speak.

Over the course of two decades, I have been a strategy consultant. During that time, I have had a front-row seat as our clients have prepared for the future. In the process, we have unleashed the value of many of these enterprises, helping them to become the best versions of themselves. Along the way, I have hoped to be half as good at what I do as Scully was at what he did.

I wrote this book because many companies are struggling to remain relevant. It appears having a killer value proposition is not good enough anymore, because every business model is under attack. By the time a company builds strategic advantage, its methods are copied by competitors who try to take those advantages away, like an outfielder snatching a ball sailing over the center-field fence.

Today there are a number of so-called strategic planning books on the market that delve deep into process but offer little in the way of strategic thinking. It is not very useful to have a strategic plan if you do not have a strategy.

No expert, thought leader or consultant should suggest that their canned solutions work for all. Preparation may look very different in a company that is product-driven than in a professional services firm.

We also get caught in a trap, where the urgent nature of today's work always takes precedence over strategy. We feel greater accomplishment from finishing routine tasks than attacking large projects that deliver enterprise value but may require months to complete.

In Part 1 of this work, we will endeavor to illuminate topics that entrepreneurs and their management teams should think about in the formation of strategy. Then, in Part 2, we will share methods best-in-class companies use to create strategic plans.

It has been in vogue in recent years for companies to write one-page business plans. It appears some management teams, in their desire to check a box, are content to fill out a form. We, too, will offer simple tools and access to templates that you can use in your business right away.

But we won't be taking any shortcuts. Simple does not mean complete. If you are looking for minimum effort, I suggest you find another book. Good strategy, like most things that are useful, requires some preparation and perspiration. We hope that you have the humility to prepare, and consider strategic planning to be worthy of your time. For a business to remain relevant over an extended period requires the kind of focus and commitment displayed by Vin Scully, day after day, night after night, year after year.

If you had to do something truly important, like design an airplane or a skyscraper, would you do it on a single page? Is your business any less important? What is the point of checking a box unless there is tangible economic value?

For example, many companies associate strategy with conducting a SWOT (strengths, weaknesses, opportunities and threats) analysis. Their executives show up at an off-site venue and create a list, void of any true thought or analysis. Then, their strategy doesn't work. As a result, they rationalize that such efforts are not worthy of the investment. Then they go back to firefighting, which feels so much easier.

The reverse can also be true. Some companies have a great strategy, but no formal systems or processes to ensure that their strategies can be implemented. We will provide the structure, but the approach in this book is much more like a gym membership than a magic bullet.

I have also found that great strategy is not something that can be rushed. Many clients have told me that their strategy retreats are a rare instance when they have time to think.

Why does strategic planning matter? The strong correlation between strategy and ROI (return on investment) is well chronicled. Bain's annual survey of senior executives ranks strategic planning as the second most important management activity (behind only customer relationship management) among initiatives that are accretive to enterprise value.

There are roughly 197,000 mid-market companies in the United States. During the Great Recession, 18 percent of them filed for bankruptcy.[1] Our company has worked with over one hundred and thirty companies. During the liquidity crisis, none of them failed.

There is of course a difference between cause and correlation. We can't, and would not, take credit for the impressive economic value that has been built by our clients. But we have borne witness to thriving growth companies that have employed the concepts that follow.

There are many things thriving companies do well, and ensuring that their management teams are on the same page (literally) is a condition that is omnipresent in best-in-breed organizations. A well-thought-out strategic plan is like the glue that binds together managers and provides inspiration to their teams. Other reasons companies engage in strategic planning are:

- To clarify a company's strategic objectives
- To set clear goals for management, to which they can be held accountable
- To prioritize investments such as the implementation of an Enterprise Resource Planning (ERP) system, or the opening of a new factory that could drain capital and resources
- To promote fact-based decision-making based on data
- To promote transparency

- To create a foundation for key performance indicators
- To provide a foundation for departmental and individual goal setting and incentive plans

Yet the real upside for having a roadmap is creating a unifying vision for an organization. A vision can be the source of universal pride, and provide a lens into the future for employees so that they can see how they are connected to something bigger than they are.

These are uncertain times, and every company needs an edge to promote value creation and sustained growth. We hope this work provides you the roadmap to frame your vision, and to realize your potential.

A NOTE TO READERS

Statistically speaking, few people will read a book cover-to-cover. We hope you will make an exception.

We assume you are very well read, and if you are, there may be some concepts to follow that you are familiar with. We hope to layer in some nuance so that you may look at things differently. Throughout the book you will see "call-outs" that highlight the most important points, which are also recapped in each chapter summary.

This book is organized into two sections. Part 1 is focused on strategy. How should a management team decide where and how to grow, and how will its value proposition resonate in the marketplace? How will your client acquisition model and marketing align with the strategy? Part 2 is more "how-to" and provides tools on how to leverage strategic planning as a management process.

Throughout this book you will find practical tools you can use to optimize your business today, and to prepare to seize the opportunities ahead.

Marc Emmer
Valencia, California

Chapter 1
BREAKING THROUGH

"The trouble with most folks isn't their ignorance.
It's knowin' so many things that ain't so."
—Josh Billings

O N A WARM OCTOBER EVENING at the 1968 Olympic
Games, the crowd waited restlessly as track and field
officials scattered, looking for a measuring tape.
A 22-year-old American, Bob Beamon, had leapt beyond the
capabilities of the automated measuring equipment designed
to track athletes in flight.

From 1960–1967 the record was broken eight times,
and had progressed by a total of 8.5 inches (or about one
inch each time the record had been set). When his jump was
first announced in meters (8.39 m), the distance of 29 feet
2½ inches confused Beamon, who did not at first understand
the enormity of his accomplishment. Upon learning that he

had shattered the world record by nearly two feet, Beamon's knees buckled, and he fainted on the track.

Beamon's jump was named by ESPN as one of the greatest sports feats of the 20th century. Beamon's record stood (remarkably) for twenty-three years. It was, literally, a giant leap for humankind.

Conditions were ideal for a world record that day. There was a significant tailwind, the maximum allowable to be included as a world record, and the rarefied air in Mexico City provided less resistance than in lower altitudes. Physicists have studied the climate at the precise moment of Beamon's jump and estimated that it may have aided him by a foot.

Beamon had executed flawlessly, and floated at a historic rate of 22 mph. As it turns out, a world-record-caliber long jump requires an ideal environment (track, temperature and wind), speed, leaping ability and a perfect launch.

> *To have the optimum business strategy requires a similar set of conditions. Great strategy requires a company to be in the right market, with the right products and services communicated in a way that resonates with customers. The strategy must then be executed well for it to work.*

Companies have a hard time leaping forward like Beamon did. Two percent of companies employ more than one hundred people.[2] Less than .004 percent of companies reach $100 million in sales. Less than a third of family businesses make it to the second generation.[3] Most businesses, at some point, hit a wall. I am the guy that helps them jump over it.

> Shockingly, companies fight against their environment all the time. When a market is flat or in decline, the only way to win business within it is to take share from rivals. Growing markets allow space for new competitors. Maintaining a healthy business requires that a company be in a growing market, be the low-cost competitor or reframe its business model to promote meaningful competitive advantage.

I have observed situations where entrepreneurs sat idly, waiting for conditions to return to the way they once were. Competitive advantage is not meaningful if it is temporary. Many industries are cyclical, but few have returned to the way things were before the Great Recession. Hyper-competition has fundamentally and permanently altered the business cycle. The prevailing winds do not suddenly just reverse themselves.

> We operate in a series of cycles: economic, monetary, political, industry, and so forth. Thus, a company's success over several decades or generations requires constant evaluation of market dynamics, strategy and positioning.

I have had a unique vantage point observing companies facing this struggle. It has been my privilege to help over 130 organizations craft their business strategies. Our firm (Optimize Inc.—*www.optimizeinc.net*) has worked with some large companies, including Justice Stores (Tween Brands), CBRE and Rio Tinto. But most of our clients have been mid-market, entrepreneurial companies (the U.S. government defines mid-market as $10 million to $1 billion in revenue).

I would make the following observation of entrepreneurs: Most nights they go to bed feeling grateful for the abundance and flexibility entrepreneurship affords them. They wake up most mornings excited to seize the opportunities ahead. In between, there are nights when they wake up in a cold sweat, petrified that they could run out of runway.

This fear is raw, and based on a universal truth: Any business worth being in will certainly draw competition. It is as if a company's core competency, the secret sauce that provided competitive advantage, is on a collision course with price compression, margin erosion and commoditization. Before the competition shows up, few companies have the wherewithal to pivot.

People will rationalize that they can't plan because the world is changing so fast. But that is actually the very reason that companies are planning more often (Jeff Bezos at Amazon conducts annual strategic planning sessions, and conducts strategy check-in sessions every Tuesday). As Mike Tyson once said, "everyone has a plan until they get punched in the mouth."

The U.S. Navy built the first satellite navigation system in 1959 after the successful launch of the Russian Sputnik satellite two years earlier. After the Russians shot down Korean Air flight 007 in 1983, President Reagan opened up the U.S. Global Positioning System (GPS) to commercial aircraft. At the time, market leader Garmin focused on providing GPS for boating and private aircraft.

In 2000 the U.S. military stopped scrambling satellite signals, opening a door for the commercial application of GPS. The new technology enabled consumer-grade navigation signals to achieve pinpoint precision, at ten times the accuracy of the existing technologies.[4] Overnight, many entrants flooded the market. Market leader Garmin lost 70 percent of its enterprise value within one year. There is a quote from a Hemingway novel to the effect that companies go bankrupt very slowly, and then very quickly.

These stories are all too familiar. Disruptive technologies and disruptive companies upset the apple cart, seemingly overnight, in industries that took decades to erect. Often, entrepreneurs find themselves in a predicament. They will either create disruption, ride industry trends or be outpaced by the rate of change.

The traditional barriers of entry have eroded. Sometimes such disruption is driven by an outside event that is beyond the control of an incumbent, as was the case with Garmin.

Garmin quickly expanded into commercial aircraft and consumer applications. It is one of the few companies to suffer such devastation in its business and fight back to become a stronger company.

Traditional companies often find themselves at a disadvantage. Startups and new entrants think of themselves as growth companies, not value companies. This is an important strategic decision every management team needs to make. Growth companies may be willing to buy businesses at low prices, because they care more about growth than profit.

Another example of traditional barriers eroding can be found in a long-lasting strategic management principle known as the "last mile of distribution," which denotes that the last mile is the most expensive. For years, this barrier of entry provided grocery and department stores with shelter from e-commerce, because it is less efficient to get goods to a consumer through methods other than retail distribution. At the Consumer Electronics Show in 2017, Mercedes demonstrated a delivery vehicle with the ability to launch drones within a neighborhood where it is parked. It won't be long before companies like UPS and FedEx will face unparalleled competition. Disruption is ubiquitous and omnipresent.

Uncertainty has been the impetus behind new business models and management practices that require companies to be nimble. The agile movement is proof positive that we are undergoing a revolution within management. However, most companies that work within mature industries also have highly entrenched management systems that cannot be undone overnight. There is something to be said for blending the learning of decades of management practices with contemporary approaches that promote agility.

We have learned this the hard way with multiple clients that have tried to embed agile principles into existing management cultures. We advocate for finding a balance of structured approaches that promote discipline and unstructured approaches that promote speed. The greater the uncertainty in an industry, the faster companies must pivot and the more likely they will adopt cutting-edge practices.

We look into the future so that we can decide what to do today. Every company has a method for strategizing, but prioritizing what we do today is critical for companies to execute their strategy well.

In business-to-business (B2B), customers are consolidating suppliers. The influence professional procurement will have in the future cannot be minimized. Customers want to work with a few select vendors who can satisfy their onerous payment terms, compliance requirements, co-managed inventory systems, quality standards and pricing preferences.

Suppliers will need to be obsessed with increasing their capabilities, not only for production but for things like cybersecurity and compliance. These customers will have fewer suppliers and will expect more from them. Some professional procurement organizations are trying to optimize their supply chains and costs; others are acting in a predatory manner in an effort to justify their existence.

In business-to-consumer (B2C), any advantages offered through distribution, or even quality, have been degraded in an omni-channel world, where consumers have access to every product in real time, at bargain basement prices. The strong will survive and the weak will go away. It is just how the world works.

B2C businesses have faced an enormous proliferation of brands and become highly fragmented. Few companies or brands can command a market leadership position over an extended period of time. For every Tide and Crest, there is a long list of companies that fail to sustain competitive advantage.

However, it is important to understand why market leaders are able to maintain their leadership.

In Apple's case, customers remain loyal because they believe the next product will be better than the last, and are unlikely to switch even if a Samsung product has new or improved features.

> 💡 To create "accumulative advantage" requires a supplier to provide a remarkable experience over an extended period of time, so the buyer doesn't make judgments based on an offer on a given day.

It is easier to be an incumbent because it is costly and difficult for customers to switch brands. In fact, neuroscience has proven that it's more physically strenuous for the brain to reconcile new information than it is for the brain to repeat a familiar pattern. Our bias is to stick with what we know.

Customers are lazy. Strong marketers capitalize on this by locking buyers into habits that they "rinse and repeat" (literally, in the case of Tide). The contemporary marketer rewards these customers through awards for repeating buying behavior, thereby creating customer loyalty. This is validated by the trend toward subscription pricing, where customers don't have to work hard to pay, even if the total cost of ownership is higher. For example, Microsoft's 365 service (at approximately $99 per year) replaced the out-of-the-box solution that cost about $399.

In B2B we see a different pattern emerging. Professional buyers needing to prove their worth will switch, even if they can only rationalize a small price difference. Then they lock in to providers they view as safe. As the old saying goes, "No one ever got fired for hiring IBM."

In the past, there was a rhythm to industry life cycles, and incumbents had time to react to new innovations offered by competitors.

Nearly two decades after GPS became available to the masses, the rate of change is happening faster than ever. Few will thrive in an age of uncertainty.

> *That's why strategy is so important. A company's business model, value proposition, strategy and tactics cannot remain static. They must be dynamic, changing with market conditions. A company's strategic plan is never complete. And in fact, strategic thinking must occur at a more rapid pace than at any time in the past.*
>
> *We will need to divest ourselves of old ideas and abandon practices that took years to develop. Companies will need to shed legacy businesses and create new muscle—that is, the ability to adapt in real time.*

Whenever I work with a management team, I ask a lot of questions to provoke thought. One of the first is "What is your end game?" For most business owners, it is to optimize the value of their asset. Sometimes this is for purposes of a liquidity event or exit for themselves, or to reward their management team or employees.

Another universal truth: More valuable companies have more options. A management team of a growing, thriving company can secure more financing, buy more equipment, hire more people, invent new technologies and so forth.

> *Although valuation methods vary by industry, most private U.S. businesses are sold for a multiple of their EBITDA (Earnings Before Interest, Taxes, Depreciation and Amortization). And clearly, larger companies are more valuable than smaller companies.*

As of this writing, the average multiple for private companies of less than $500 million was around ten times their earnings.[5] Meanwhile, public companies are trading at over twenty times their earnings.

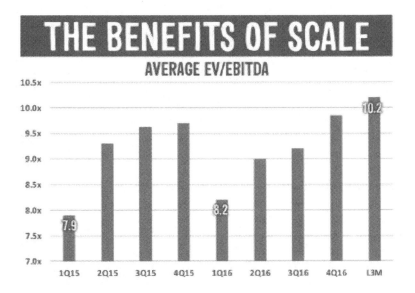

THE BENEFITS OF SCALE
AVERAGE EV/EBITDA

There is a sweet spot for valuation at over $5 million EBITDA, because that is when private equity becomes interested in a business. Including more buyers (such as private equity) in an auction (or more focused sell-side process) drives up valuation. Multiples of smaller companies are much lower—often as low as four or five times EBITDA.

> *Size matters for other reasons. Larger companies absorb overhead at a faster rate (over more volume). Larger customers want their suppliers to be highly capable and will leverage their pricing power to take advantage of smaller suppliers. Larger companies fail at a lesser rate in downturns than smaller ones. Most smart entrepreneurs I know view growth as a mandate for survival.*

In an age of professional procurement, customers expect their suppliers to have little concentration risk—that they as a customer do not make up too large a portion of total volume. In annual reviews, such ratios are part of the ongoing evaluation of suppliers. In other words, companies have to grow just to keep the customers they already have.

Growth is a function of having the best offer and communicating it better than anyone else. In B2B environments, suppliers have a hard time creating differentiation. We endeavor in these pages to provide practical tools that companies can use to "break the tie" in the many situations where the varying attributes of vendors are indistinguishable by customers.

This new era will require best-in-breed sales and marketing engines. Providers must be fanatical about providing value, because value is a moving target.

> *There is an inherent conflict between profit and growth. Management teams focused on value creation understand the "size premium" and naturally reinvest proceeds back into the business to expand their reach. To reinvest proceeds is the impetus of building enterprise value over time.*
>
> *If your business is worth six times its EBITDA, the management team's goal should be to get to seven or eight times EBITDA.*

Our firm has identified ten Value Drivers that business owners should focus on to achieve their maximum value:

1. Diversified Markets and Customers
2. Business Model and Sustainable Revenue Model
3. Unique Value Proposition and Branding that Proves Value
4. Financial Health
5. Sales Competency and Customer Relationships
6. Right People in the Right Seats
7. Leadership and Culture
8. Technology and Information
9. Scalability and Service Excellence
10. Planning and Execution

Throughout the book we examine each of these topics and translate them into tangible activities.

We have worked with many high-growth companies. In a period where GNP growth has been tepid, high-growth companies must constantly evolve their business models to maintain such trajectories. For a company to grow at 10 percent requires that it expand at roughly four to five times the growth of GNP. This is a tall order.

Some managers have told me they don't want to grow; they're fine where they are. I call *bullshit*. Today's business environment does not tolerate a company growing at a rate slower than its competition or industry. When a business doesn't generate enough cash to do more than it did before, it doesn't take long to fall behind in technology or the war for talent. One of my clients is a former engineering professor who has run an industry-leading business for over fifty years. In his words, "A successful company is a growing company."

> *The principles outlined in this work are for those committed to increasing enterprise value through sustainable, profitable growth over the long term.*

I have also had managers rationalize why their business can't grow. If a business can't grow, it is usually because it is in the wrong market, or doesn't have a differentiated offer. Management teams that allow such circumstances to persist are putting their companies at risk.

The E-Myth books, *Good to Great* and many other management volumes have chronicled that companies have difficulty
managing their life cycle. Within our work, we have touched
every conceivable corner of the economy, and just about every
industry vertical. The rules of competition apply to all, and
the pains and opportunity presented by life cycle are a reality
we witness daily.

Once a company reaches a point of scale—let's say $20
to $50 million for the sake of discussion—it requires profes-
sional management and systems to grow. A controller is no
longer adequate; the company needs a real CFO. Systems that
were cobbled together do not provide the CFO with adequate
financial data or business intelligence. The company needs to
invest in an ERP.

But the IT director is the guy who once fixed the copiers
and has no experience deploying such complex systems. The
sales leader is an old-school relationship manager and does
not really understand managing a pipeline and wouldn't be
caught dead with a Customer Relationship Management
(CRM) System.

During this stage of the life cycle, the entrepreneur's bandwidth becomes very limiting. Because of these pain points, the
technicians and inventors who started businesses get stuck being
operators. Entrepreneurs do not have the time to manage the
day-to-day of their business, and to consider transformation at
the same time. We refer to this as the "entrepreneur's dilemma."[6]

---

*It is easy for an entrepreneur to become a
slave to her business, and lose touch with the*

artistry that made her great. She loses her ability to see around the bend. When entrepreneurs are stuck in the day-to-day operations of their business, it is impossible for them to tweak their service delivery and business models in a way that provides the differentiating advantages required to stay relevant.

To break through from $20 million to $50 million, or from $50 million to $100 million requires management to adapt a radically different mindset. These companies tread water until they bite the bullet: They pay the CFO $200,000, a number that seemed inconceivable just two years earlier. He demands to see a strategic plan. He provides real financial reporting and intelligence. He negotiates a credit line with a bank that promotes growth. The same breakthroughs occur in HR, IT, engineering, and so forth.

Companies move to being professionally managed when their leaders transition from tactical thinking to managing growth, business models, strategy and economic value. There is a direct and linear relationship between enterprise value and the ability to hire professionals who think in these terms.

"A" players hire other "A" players, whereas "B" players hire "B" and "C" players. It is only after making this transition that a company can begin to accumulate better talent and extend beyond the ability of the entrepreneur.

People have a hard time managing the status quo, and seeing what it is that could replace it. Such lieutenants are not huge risk-takers. Often their incentive plans reward profit, but not investment in research and development. Typically, incentive plans are tied to EBITDA. This creates an inequity where a management team can be paid based on the upside of R&D but doesn't participate in the risk.

The entrepreneur's dilemma implies that entrepreneurs need to entrust the day-to-day operation of a business to other people (or be operators and hire others to have a vision, do the R&D and more). Because many entrepreneurs are also inventors and tinkerers, they have an even harder time delegating innovation than they do operational control. The entrepreneur's dilemma is exacerbated by the fact that many entrepreneurs are bad delegators.

For a company to create an edge requires there to be constant exploration. But the skill sets required for innovation are diametrically opposed to those required for executing well within a core market.

According to a study published in the *Harvard Business Review*, fewer than 2 percent of firms have the competencies to execute both well.[7]

It is not that growing a core business and transforming it are in competition with one another; it is that they are in direct conflict.

DIFFERING COMPETENCIES

CORE

Short-term
Efficiency
Discipline
Clarity of direction
Internal focus
Productivity focus

EXPLORATION

Long-term
Innovation
Flexible adaptation
Empowerment
External focus
Growth focus

~2%
of firms

So where and how is a company to grow? The classic definition of strategy is to decide which battles to fight. Defining the optimal scope of a business is perhaps the most important strategic decision a management team makes.

Gaining momentum at the right time is a huge factor in building enterprise value. Legendary football coach Bill Belichick sparked a trend in the National Football League by "deferring" (not taking the ball after winning the coin toss). Teams that defer win about 60 percent of the time. With regularity the New England Patriots score on their last possession of the first half, then regain the ball to start the second half. With more information than they would have at the beginning of a game, the Patriots seize the momentum, scoring back-to-back at a pivotal part of the game.

Luck is also a factor in strategy. Sometimes business owners end up in the right place at the right time. If you watch competitive poker on television, you know that the professionals win most of the hands and almost all the tournaments. Although there is luck in poker, good card players play the percentages and put themselves in a position to win. In business, riding the wave of a strong market is a higher percentage play than hoping for a market to reverse course. Thus the old saying, *Hope is not a strategy.*

For some inexplicable reason, companies do not spend much time researching the perfect environment in which to operate and therefore don't benefit from being in an optimal environment as Beamon did. They spend a lot of time figuring out how to maximize the business they are already in.

> *In large part this work is about breaking through barriers to growth, and developing the perfect offer, in the best environment, supported by the resources required to scale profitability. It is about helping management teams manage the tension between doing what they already do well and the need to venture out. It is about developing an accumulative advantage that promotes momentum.*

There is an important distinction between accumulated advantage and competitive advantage. Competitive advantage implies the best offer at a fixed point in time. Accumulative advantage promotes a reputation over an extended period, which insulates incumbents from new entrants that may rely on discounting their offers.

Finally, companies must have a method for sharing their fanaticism with employees who buy into either vision. There is a battle of generational forces underfoot; boomers perceive millennials as divorced from the former's way of thinking (I am a boomer, with the salt-and-pepper hair to prove it). Legacy companies will need to undergo a paradigm shift to connect with a new generation of workers who will carry our businesses and our legacies into the future.

Today, more than 50 percent of procurement people are millennials. They are not only the buyers of tomorrow; they will be the executive managers and decision makers of the future.

I once had the following exchange with a millennial. I said, "People of my generation think that people of your generation would rather look at their phone than talk to us." He said, "Well, sometimes the phone is more interesting than the person you are talking to." This sentiment reflects a shift in how people think and how we must evolve to meet the needs of buyers, including the decision makers of the future.

In the past, customers wanted to meet us; today millennials want to read about us on the internet. There is an important distinction between creating value and communicating it. We will offer insights on how to create the game-changing value proposition, and communicate it in a way that engages the prospective buyers of tomorrow.

The greatest wealth is built in periods of chaos. Everyone reading these pages has the opportunity to pivot and put their companies in a position to win. To gain momentum requires hard work, the right people, the right product and a willingness to fail.

So read on, and be prepared to think differently about strategy formation and your company's place in the new world order. It is time to build momentum.

CHAPTER REVIEW

▶ To have the optimum business strategy requires an optimum set of conditions. Great strategy requires that a company be in the right market, with the right products and services, communicating in a way that resonates with customers. Then its strategy must be executed well for it to work.

▶ Companies fight against their environment all the time. When a market is flat or in decline, the only way to win business within it is to take share from rivals. Growing markets allow space for new competitors.

▶ We operate in a series of cycles—economic, monetary, political, industry and so forth. Thus, for a company to succeed over a decade or more requires constant evaluation of market dynamics, strategy and positioning.

▶ To create "accumulative advantage" requires a supplier to provide a remarkable experience over an extended period of time.

- A company's business model, value proposition, strategy and tactics cannot be static. They must be dynamic, changing with market conditions. A company's strategic plan is never complete. And in fact, strategic thinking must occur at a quicker pace than ever before.

- We will need to divest ourselves of old ideas and abandon practices that have taken years to develop.

- Size matters for several reasons. Larger companies absorb overhead at a faster rate (over more volume). Larger customers want to do business with larger suppliers and will leverage their pricing power with smaller suppliers.

- There is an inherent conflict between profit and growth. Management teams focused on value creation understand the "size premium" and naturally reinvest proceeds back into the business.

- If your business is worth six times its EBITDA, the management team's goal should be to get to seven or eight times EBITDA. Our firm has identified ten Value Categories that business owners should focus on to achieve their optimum value (highlighted throughout the book).

- The principles outlined in this work are for those committed to increasing enterprise value through sustainable, profitable growth over the long term.

- Companies move to being professionally managed when their leaders transition from tactical thinking to managing growth, business models, strategy and economic value. There is a linear relationship between the ability of a business to hire such professionals and its success.

▸ It is easy for an entrepreneur to become a slave to the business and lose touch with the artistry that made him or her great.

▸ Growing a core business and transforming it are not in competition with one another—they are in direct conflict.

Chapter 2
GROWTH AND DIVERSIFICATION

"I tell everyone in our business, you should wake up every morning terrified with your sheets drenched in sweat, but not because you're afraid of our competitors. Be afraid of our customers because those are the folks who have the money."

—Jeff Bezos, Amazon CEO

ETER DRUCKER ONCE FAMOUSLY asked Jack Welch, "If you weren't already in this business, would you enter it today?" I have often used this question as a barometer. If you could reinvent your business from scratch, what would it look like? If you needed to separate from the pack, would you make incremental improvements or do something radically different?

If one were to oversimplify it, there are three primary ways you can grow a business: in your core market, in adjacent products and markets, or in ways that are "transformational" or "disruptive." As published in the *Harvard Business Review* (HBR) article "Managing Your Innovation Portfolio" authors Nagji and Tuff conducted a study that measured the "innovation ambitions" of companies. That is, they measured the proportion of investment (as measured by their growth initiatives) in core, adjacent and transformational pursuits. One could think of the study as measuring an entrepreneur's risk tolerance as it relates to innovation.

Nagji and Tuff's research revealed a disproportionate return on capital realized by companies that invest 70 percent in core, 20 percent in adjacencies and 10 percent in disruption. Famously, this is the proportion of investment allocated by Google. Larry Page, Google's cofounder, cites the 70/20/10 formula as a key contributor to the company's success.

GROWTH PORTFOLIO

70/20/10

Not all companies should employ a 70/20/10 formula, but every management team should have one. The HBR study revealed that there is an inverse relationship to the return on such investments, that the 10 percent of investment in transformation yielded 70 percent of economic value in the long term, with 70 percent of short-term results coming from core. We refer to this model as a "growth portfolio."

Many companies say they think strategically, but actually keep doing what they have always done, which is not strategy at all. To put all our eggs in one basket is inherently risky. So a growth portfolio of 100/0/0 is not very sustainable, unless your core market grows at a healthy rate into perpetuity. Almost every market eventually becomes commoditized. If you think that is unlikely in your market, you might as well collect unicorns as a business model.

This behavior is easy to understand if you think about the underlying psychology. To innovate and do something new requires an admission that what was done before may not have been the best course of action. It is human nature to seek out confirmation that we have already made the right decision (confirmation bias). As a U.S. Defense Secretary once put it, we face known-knowns, known-unknowns and unknown-unknowns. Our inability to predict unknown-unknowns can cause us to be "unexpectedly wrong."[8]

It is for this reason that companies must pursue smart diversification (unless they have evidence that supports doubling down in their core). Markets are just too unstable and unpredictable to know exactly when they will implode. The resulting price compression and margin erosion become a self-fulfilling prophecy. The need to diversify puts us in conflict with the knowledge that the incremental cost to sell an existing client a new product or service is typically much lower than acquiring a new customer or entering a new market.

It is the job of the management team to assess a core market in relation to other potential markets and/or investment alternatives. Only after such an assessment can a management team know if its core market is the right one to focus on in the future.

VALUE DRIVER:
DIVERSIFIED MARKETS AND CUSTOMERS

Value Driver Tip—Achieve diversification in markets and customers. Companies should aspire to have no less than 40 percent of volume in any vertical or geographic market and no more than 15 percent of volume with any one customer.

It is critical that such decisions be based on data. Two of the most important data points are industry size and growth rate. A business in a flat market can grow only through taking share from competitors.

Disruption is coming to every industry. Entrants such as Square, the Khan Academy and Waze tend to enter markets violently and suddenly.

A trap many management teams fall into is that they associate innovation with new products. Business model innovation is under-leveraged as a strategy tool.

Our client, Kravitz, has been a third-party administrator of retirement plans since the '70s. Founder Lou Kravitz was a pioneer, serving as an advisor to the Internal Revenue Service and formulating rules governing his industry.

His son Dan took over the helm just before the Great Recession and at a time when the company faced an inflection point. Third-party administrators were facing a period of rapid commoditization, and the average Kravitz fee had plateaued.

Dan and his team made several key decisions that would reshape the company. He hired our firm to conduct annual strategic planning sessions and made it known that he wanted annual meetings to include discussions of potential opportunities that could transform the business.

Dan felt strongly that the company needed to find a point of difference. Management decided to focus on "cash balance" plans, a narrow segment of the retirement plan market. Cash balance plans are valued in companies that pass certain IRS hurdles, and thus the target market was too small for large providers that typically focus on the mass market. Niche businesses tend not to draw in large competitors.

Once clients decided to add a cash balance plan, they often wanted advice on investments. Kravitz had created a retirement plan advisory. But the company's investment arm had no place to park its clients' assets, since no funds targeted to cash balance plans existed at the time. So one of Kravitz's big bets was to start a cash balance mutual fund (Payden/ Kravitz fund).

In another year, the Kravitz management team took another problem and turned it into an opportunity. The company didn't have enough scale to employ a large sales force. Other third-party administrators (TPAs) did not know much about the cash balance market, and many did not have the actuaries required to manage the intricacies of complying with federal law. Kravitz offered up an online portal where other TPAs could sell cash balance plans to their clients by leveraging the Kravitz back end. In effect, by making the technology available, Kravitz accessed the sales resources of its competitors.

In another year, Kravitz made another big bet. Emerging as a leader in the cash balance space, Dan coauthored a book with two salespeople. At conferences or industry events, any one of the three could be announced as the author. They also created a video series to sell to other TPAs so that those TPAs would use the Kravitz portal. Kravitz was positioned as the clear thought leader in the space.

After many years of strategic planning, making one major strategic bet at a time, Kravitz emerged as the market leader (as measured in number of plans/participants) of cash balance plans in the United States. The mutual fund surpassed $200 million under management. Further, the company built a vertically integrated platform, with many profit centers—consulting, investment advisory, mutual fund, online webinars and Kravitz Back Office Solutions.

When we started working with Kravitz, it had about forty-five employees. Today it has about ninety. Kravitz is an example of a company that has "broken through" barriers by radically shifting a business model. A company of any size can break through to the next level utilizing this way of thinking.

What Kravitz did successfully was to understand its place in the value chain, and extend into services above and below its traditional position. It took about eight years, but Kravitz chipped away at innovation until it had completely transformed from a struggling TPA into a service platform. In 2017 a strategic buyer acquired the business, validating that Kravitz had created meaningful economic value.

> *To remain relevant, companies must understand where they "live" in the value chain (as Kravitz did). As evidenced in this example, true insight into a business and evaluation of the value chain is not just for large companies; it is applicable to companies of all shapes and sizes.*
>
> *When companies are "one-trick ponies," offering one service in one sector, they may thrive in the short term as specialists, but they, too, are subject to price competition and commoditization. Companies that can expand beyond their initial offering and get their hooks deeper into a client will improve stickiness.*

A fully integrated company participating in a broad range of activities in the value chain is known as a platform or network company.

A "platform" may include various services on the periphery of a core service. Although customers will fight for pennies when negotiating price on a core service, there is far less price sensitivity for peripheral services. It is extremely unlikely that a buyer will "shop" such ancillary services.

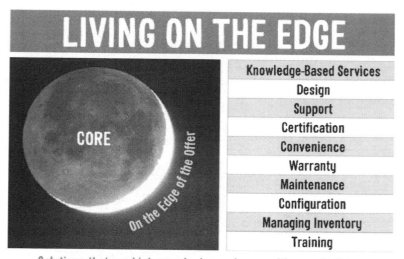

LIVING ON THE EDGE

CORE	Knowledge-Based Services
On the Edge of the Offer	Design
	Support
	Certification
	Convenience
	Warranty
	Maintenance
	Configuration
	Managing Inventory
	Training

Solutions that are high margin, less price sensitive, and sticky. They leverage "foundational assets".

In addition to being higher profit, such services provide further stickiness to a product, and do so only at limited incremental cost.[9] This is because a provider can leverage existing "foundational" assets in the delivery of such services, which can include warranties, configuration fees and certifications.

Sellers should capitalize on maximizing such services before expanding into new markets (which are riskier).

Many of the most valuable companies in the world today—including Apple, Amazon, eBay and Uber—are platform companies. Although entrepreneurial companies may not have the scale to be platform providers, there are attributes commonly found in platform companies that smaller companies can employ to expand their participation in the value chain. The Kravitz story proves that platform attributes can apply to modest-size service companies.

There are a number of attributes common in platform companies:

- Seamless Transactions. The ability to complete a transaction easily and instantly
- Education. The ability to offer or sell knowledge
- Co-Revenue. Sharing revenue with customers or alliance partners
- Radical Pricing. Offering a radically different pricing model
- Personalization. Ability to customize to suit (such as the shirt maker Proper Cloth)
- Asset Sharing. Shared utilization of assets (such as Airbnb)
- Usage-Based Pricing. Paying for only what you use
- Collaborative Ecosystem. Collaboration across the supply chain
- Agile Organization. Faster decision making
- Scalability. The ability to complete an unlimited number of transactions at little incremental cost

We can see how often such attributes are leveraged in some of the most valuable companies in our economy:

PLATFORM ATTRIBUTES

	Personalization	Asset Sharing	Usage Based	Collaborative	Co-Revenue	Seamless Transactions
Airbnb	X	X		X	X	X
Amazon	X		X	X	X	X
Apple	X		X	X	X	X
Salesforce	X	X	X			
Uber	X	X	X	X	X	X
Zipcar	X	X	X			X

There are over 250,000 landscaping companies in the United States. Of those companies, our client Gothic Landscape ranks tenth in revenue. Gothic's core business has historically been landscaping new housing developments (construction). Construction is a notoriously cyclical business. During down-cycles, builders pull back and play a cat-and-mouse game with their contractors. Pricing power can shift at any moment.

To mitigate huge shifts in demand and pricing power, Gothic decided to build a maintenance division. Once communities are built out, the maintenance business could service clients on an ongoing basis. This proved to be a crucial strategic decision, not only because the company diversified its revenue but because the company now has different competencies and cost structures that better align with customer needs. The construction division "turns over" projects to maintenance, creating inherent synergies and lower customer acquisition costs.

During downturns such as the Great Recession, many poorly capitalized landscape companies folded. Gothic was able to sustain cash flow through its maintenance contracts and achieved strong financial results. During the recovery it was in a position to grow again (albeit in a slow housing recovery with very tight margins) in the construction business.

Kravitz and Gothic both started in the right niche market and expanded as specialists into multiple disciplines. Thus there is something between being a specialist and a generalist: A company can be a multi-market specialist.

High-growth companies can easily crawl into a concentration trap. There is an opportunity cost, where pursuing new customers is at the expense of existing ones. This is often seen when account managers are also responsible for new client acquisition. It is always easier to serve an existing customer than to break into a new market.

Often, the largest customers are the ones growing the most. Imagine a $50 million company, with a $5 million customer growing at 10 percent. If the company retained 90 percent of its remaining revenue base and grew it 5 percent, and brought in $4 million in new revenue, its new concentration would be as follows:

	Year 1	Year 2
Client A Revenue	$5.0 M	$5.5 M
Other Retained Business	$45.0 M	$42.5 M
Other New Business		$4.0 M
Total	$50.0 M	$52.0 M
Client A Share	10.0%	10.6%

In this scenario, Client A's business is now 10.6 percent of revenue and client concentration (with the one client) has increased. Providers can find themselves in the unenviable position of having to intentionally slow down growth for their largest customers. The only way to grow organically and crawl out of the concentration trap is to overinvest in growth in less valuable customers or in client acquisition.

Revenue diversification can be achieved through organic growth, acquisition or development of new business segments. A company's growth portfolio may not be 70/20/10, but it is important that every company recognize its risks and opportunities in core and non-core business and invest accordingly.

Among the most difficult decisions management teams face are build, buy and rent decisions. Acquisitions are the fastest method for achieving diversification.

Acquisitions can also be a crutch. When low-growth companies seek out acquisition as a "growth strategy," they are indicating their inability to grow organically. If they fold in (or bolt on) similar companies, ones that are also struggling to grow (which is often the case with divested companies), they only perpetuate the problem. If financing is required to execute such a transaction, the buyer has a bigger beast to feed and higher costs as a result of debt service. The grass is not always greener on the other side.

Perhaps this is why Fortune 1000 companies are having such a hard time realizing synergies promised in acquisitions. A 2016 study by KPMG listed the top motivations for buyers:

Expand customer base	37%
Enter into new lines of business	37%
Expand geographic reach	36%
Enhance intellectual property or acquire new technologies	34%
Opportunistic—target becomes available	25%
Financial buyer looking for profitable operations and/or gain on exit	20%
Invest in another function in the supply chain	16%
Respond to activist investor	13%
Defend against competition	7%

These results show two very different pathways for acquisitions and build, buy or rent decisions.

Some companies are buying for strategic reasons, such as entering a new line of business (adjacent or transformational) or expanding geographic reach (adjacency). Thirty-seven percent are buying companies for their customers. This feels like a risky proposition, especially given that in most PE deals, it is assumed that 20 to 30 percent of customers are at risk.

Vertical integration, or investing in another function in the supply chain, could be considered an adjacent or transformational business. Enhancing intellectual property or acquiring new technologies is typically transformative. These are also transactions that tend to yield high multiples.

It is important that companies considering acquisitions have specific objectives and clear build-or-buy parameters. For example, we consult with service companies with strong systems and processes whose infrastructure could easily scale into new markets. Imagine a framing contractor in Tampa, Florida, deciding to enter markets in Atlanta or Miami. These would represent bolt-on acquisitions in adjacent geographies and would be easy to integrate.

However, suppose a framing contractor wanted to purchase a small lumber operation (vertical integration). Although this may be an adjacent business in some respects, the integration would be tricky because the acquirer's systems and processes would not apply. Say the contractor had an ERP system. It might not be configured to a manufacturing operation and could take a year and millions of dollars to modify.

Also, the acquirer may not have competency in the new business. This implies that the acquired company would likely keep most of its management intact. Thus the acquirer would not realize the cost synergies that are often expected in such a transaction.

A study conducted by PricewaterhouseCoopers illustrated the percentage of time when the objectives of acquisitions are realized by an acquirer. When the focal point of the acquisition was to access revenue enhancing activities, the likelihood of achieving the objective was higher than when focused on cost reduction.[10]

A popular business strategy today is to "roll-up" industries. This results in fewer, more capable, larger companies with enough revenue to remain relevant. Companies employing this strategy are attempting to participate in a form of financial arbitrage, which is also known as financial engineering. By buying smaller companies at four or five times multiple, they tack on volume to create an eight-to-nine times multiple (for example). Although this strategy appears sound on its face, failure to consider the variables described above can be crippling given the ominous nature of integrations. In a roll-up, completing acquisitions must become a core competency.

So, *caveat emptor* (let the buyer beware). Given the speed of change and risk, management teams need to be mindful of sectors with volatile industry cycles, high capital requirements and poor operating cash cycles.

As mentioned, diversification can offer more riches and greater execution risk. Consider the venerable brand Royal Philips as a case in point. In the 2000s the company secured more patents than any other in Europe.

As the company began to diversify its global portfolio, it allowed its business leaders to develop "standalone" systems and processes in support of new businesses. There was redundancy in invoicing and other systems; in some cases customers had to enter the same information in multiple systems. Products cannibalized other products.

In other words, the drive to offer variety can also create value-destroying complexity. Companies can become "addicted to innovation" at the expense of the customer experience.

When considering diversification strategies, providers should be hyper-focused on ensuring that the addition of potential volume does not disrupt the existing business. In fact, the best innovations are both enhancing and additive. For example, for a fee, software companies regularly develop new features at the request of customers and then bundle those features into an existing product, which is then marketed as a new release.

As illustrated by Kravitz, companies should search for complementary products and services that can be integrated to enrich a value proposition. Be aware of your growth portfolio, the relationship of the products and services you offer and the resources required to manage them.

Diversification is a lot like chocolate—you don't want too much, and you don't want too little.

CHAPTER REVIEW

- ▶ It is the job of the management team to assess a core market in relation to other potential markets and/or investment alternatives. Only after such an assessment will management know if its core market is the best one to focus on in the future.

▸ It is critical that such decisions be based on data. Two of the most important data points are industry size and growth rate. A business in a flat market can grow only through taking share from another company, and it will likely have to do it at a lower price. Conversely, growing markets typically have room to accept more competition.

▸ To remain relevant, companies must understand where they "live" in the value chain.

▸ When companies are one-trick ponies, offering one service in one sector, they may thrive in the short term as specialists, but are eventually subject to price competition and commoditization.

▸ Acquisitions can also be a crutch. When low-growth companies seek out acquisitions as a "growth strategy," they are admitting their inability to grow organically. If they fold in or bolt on similar companies, ones which are also struggling to grow, and this is often the case with divested companies, they only perpetuate the problem. If financing is required to execute such a transaction, the buyer now has a bigger beast to feed and higher costs as a result of debt service. The grass is not always greener on the other side.

Chapter 3
THE SWEET SPOT

"Once we over-learn something,
we cease to know it anymore at all."
—Youngme Moon

AM BORED.

I am bored by uninspired food in average restaurants.
I am bored by seeing 107 toothpaste brands in look-alike packaging in grocery stores that are indistinguishable from one another. I suffer when I look at the websites of manufacturing companies that list their products void of any points of difference. The sameness in our economy makes me want to heave.

Every business has a choice: Be the low-cost leader or be differentiated. Every marketer reading these pages understands the implications of being the former.

> 💡 One thing about the race to the bottom is that everybody loses.

Of course, there can only be one low-cost leader in every category, and most small and even mid-market companies don't have the wherewithal to compete on price.

Entire sectors of the economy take on a sameness in their trade show booths, website design, brochures, sales teams and so forth.

This conventional wisdom manifests in what I refer to as the cadence of competition. This cadence often drives competitive herding, where entire industries move in a common direction, offering the same features and benefits.

> 💡 Competitive herding is a consequence of entire industries taking on a cadence of competition. The more crowded a market, the more difficult it is to point out a brand's unique characteristics.

Commoditization occurs when a customer no longer requires maximum performance (from a product) and is willing to substitute a lower-cost alternative. Executives complain to me that their industries are commoditized and nothing can be done to create space between them and their competition.

In poker such an indicator is called a "tell." The prices a company charges are a measuring stick for its ability to deliver unique value. The market votes with its wallet every day. Executives who allow their companies to fall victim to commoditization are contributing to their eventual decline.

Yet I fervently believe that every company can turn around its value proposition and offer profound value. Later in this chapter I will provide insight on how to infuse life into a value proposition. But first we need to better explore how companies and their products/services come to be what they are.

In her excellent book, *Different,* Harvard Business School professor Youngme Moon tells the tale of the typical industry life cycle:

"When a product category is nascent, it tends to be dominated by a much smaller product line, or even a single product (like the original PowerBar or Walkman). As the category evolves, the number of product alternatives within the category tend to grow exponentially. As the number of products within a category multiplies, the differences between them start to become increasingly trivial, almost to the point of preposterousness. In these categories, there is a proliferation of sameness, rather than differentiation. They become masters of a form of imitation, not differentiation, but imitation."

The classic struggle today is for management teams to define scope:

- How many products or services should we offer?
- How many verticals or industries should we serve?
- How can we maintain a leadership position in the markets we participate in?
- Should we serve a few needs of the many, or the many needs of a few?

A function of hyper-competition is the emergence of hyper-segmentation. Although some companies are offering more, others, often referred to as reverse brands, are offering less. Before a management team can expect a sales team to target customers, there must be complete clarity on the specific market segments that should be serviced and with what offer.

The shrewd marketer is keenly aware of what tradeoffs the market is likely to accept. Every feature in a product or component in a service bundle has an opportunity cost. That is, there is a cost of offering a feature or benefit that could be invested in another feature or benefit. Customers pay a premium for a feature to be included in the product.

In a hypercompetitive market where some customers will settle for "just good enough," suppliers must know which features to strip out and at what incremental cost. Famously, Apple continues to strip its MacBook of technologies that were once expected (CD players and USB ports) as new technologies leapfrog the ones they have replaced. When search was first adopted as a service, Google won over Yahoo with a stripped down page design that offered no content. As Woody Guthrie once said, "Any fool can make something complicated. It takes a genius to make it simple."

Garmin's history shines a light on the dilemma faced by management teams running out of runway. It is well understood that specialists can provide greater depth and value to a market than generalists. Conventional wisdom dictates that specialists are better shielded from price competition. I would know; my firm, Optimize Inc., does only one thing—strategic planning—and we do it really well. Of course it is not good enough just to be different; your differentiating strategies must also be valuable. (See the Value Chain analysis in Chapter 4.)

Yet being a specialist operating in a limited number of verticals, as Garmin was, also boxes a company in and exposes it to concentration risk. Concentration risk (whether it be client concentration or industry concentration) is one of the first things buyers will look for in their efforts to devalue a potential acquisition candidate's multiple.

Specialists are at great risk should their area of specialty suffer sudden or unexpected market changes beyond their control. For example, the sudden decline in the oil and gas sector propelled 232 oil patch companies into bankruptcy in 2016 (representing $74 billion in debt[11]).

Companies achieve economies of scale by producing more pieces of a thing: buying raw materials more cheaply, automating processes and absorbing overhead over more volume. Economies of scope are realized when a company can produce multiple products and spread costs across a family of products.

So—what is the right number of products to offer or markets to serve? Specialists must choose a dimension in which to specialize. A specialist could focus on a marketplace or a service. For example, Kravitz offers many services within the one market it specializes in: cash balance plans.

My firm offers one service, but we are industry agnostic, meaning that our service can be utilized by a client in any industry.

	Product A	Product B	Product C	Product D	Product E
Market A					
Market B					
Market C					
Market D					
Market E					

To grow effectively a company could expand vertically or horizontally (along the X or Y axis). Kravitz can concentrate on industry trade shows and marketing in a singular market. As a strategy practitioner I am not a threat to other consultants, for example, leadership coaches or process improvement specialists. We are natural referral sources to each other because our niches are clearly defined. (A generalist would try to fill these roles.)

Where a company gets in trouble is when it tries to check too many boxes in the grid. Management teams must make brutally difficult decisions about the scope and breadth of their offer, understanding that there is a tradeoff between what is gained by entering new markets versus the economies of participating in very few.

At some point in the product life cycle, expansion comes from:

- Augmentation by addition; or
- Augmentation by multiplication.

Augmentation by addition occurs when a provider attempts to add features to a product or service. Augmentation by multiplication occurs when the seller offers more variations of a similar product, for example, brand extensions. Neither augmentation by addition nor by multiplication ensures sustainability. Unless there is significant growth in a category, industry players just slice up the category across more products, decreasing the performance for every component within it.

Consider the B2B application of augmentation. Widget Maker A offers a 72-hour lead time. Widget Maker B follows suit and then ups the ante by offering forward distribution, storing inventory closer to the customer. Now its lead time is 48 hours and Widget Maker A has lost its competitive advantage. In an age of professional procurement, many of the services provided by sellers become expected and only add incremental cost for every supplier.

Technology is promoting economies of scope to provide opportunities for mass-customization, which really is the midpoint between generalization and customization. This is the rage in fashion, where companies such as Trunk Club—yes, even men can buy clothing online—offer customized services around mass-produced products.

Thus, the companies that will scale while delivering value will be oriented toward providing customers with choices and service but in a model that promotes scale. When Clayton Christensen first introduced the concept of "disruptive innovation," this was the model he professed. In his definition of disruption, a technology needed to scale to become the preferred solution and fend off competitive pressures.

Executives tell me the market sets their prices, especially in B2B where professional buyers are more educated about their options. Perhaps that's true; however, it's important to note that price is also a function of circumstances and usage.

Consider the cost of cola. If you buy a Coke at a restaurant you may expect to pay $4 for twelve ounces, or 33 cents an ounce. At a vending machine, it will cost you $1.50 per can (or 13 cents an ounce), and at home you'll spend $2.59 for a 2-liter bottle, or around 4 cents an ounce. At a restaurant, the same person pays nine times what they pay at home for the same product. So what a customer is willing to pay is based on his or her motivation and circumstances.

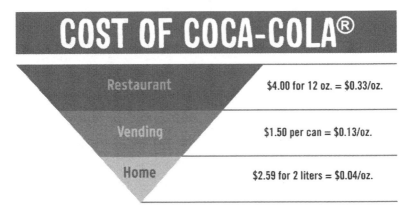

COST OF COCA-COLA®

Restaurant	$4.00 for 12 oz. = $0.33/oz.
Vending	$1.50 per can = $0.13/oz.
Home	$2.59 for 2 liters = $0.04/oz.

In B2B, many suppliers manage pricing poorly. For example, an aerospace parts manufacturer may be asked to bid on parts without knowing what plane the part is being made for. As we will explore later, the problem in this case is not with the customer or the part, but the nature of the relationship between the customer and their supplier. Customers often request rush jobs or change orders. These demands could justify additional fees, which are rarely captured by suppliers, who may be too afraid to challenge their buyers at a time they are needed most.

I have heard every conceivable rationalization on why companies cannot innovate and reframe their value proposition. *We are too small; Our industry is too old; There is too much competition.* Yet all large companies have one thing in common: They were once small companies. To become large, they beat the competition.

> *Industries are not commoditized; non-differentiated brands and products are.*

As customers become fussier and ever more skeptical, providers can attempt to satisfy smaller slivers of a market. The emerging need to hyper-segment is well illustrated by comparing the lifestyles of two very similar people. I have a dear friend who lives in New York City. He fancies designer watches, fine wine, trendy men's lotions and guitars. We grew up in the same neighborhood and have been the best of friends for 40 years. We are of the same religion and the same age. And yet what we consume could not be more different. I prefer peaty scotch, hoppy beer, the NFL and golf. (I do not have an addictive personality but I have met my match in golf. When it comes to that sport I might as well be smoking crack, eating Skittles and drinking Boone's Farm.)

B2C marketers understand hyper-segmentation all too well and are profiling their customers to understand their latent needs. Marketers are becoming astute at understanding the demographics and psychographics that inform shopping behavior. Many are even profiling what customers look like and developing personas like "Marty, the metrosexual, urban early adopter who loves dogs."

B2B providers would be well advised to follow a similar script and understand exactly why customers choose them. They will define niches very narrowly, own those niches and move on to the next as they run out of runway.

A fundamental understanding of why customers buy is critical in forming a unique value proposition. In many of my speeches I conduct an exercise in which I ask several members of one management team to step forward. I ask them to write three to four reasons why their customers make various buying decisions and which purchase triggers inform their choice. Surprisingly, there are a wide range of responses. Either the executives don't know why their customers buy, or they weigh certain purchase triggers differently than their colleagues do.

In the *Harvard Business Review* article, "The Elements of Value," writers Almquist, Senior and Bloch offer a model for how consumers evaluate products. We have adapted that model into a business-to-business framework, which we have titled "The B2B Value Pyramid." Most readers of this book will be B2B managers, and we have organized this exercise to suit.

Your team can utilize the B2B Value Pyramid to build consensus on what attributes should be represented in your competencies, branding, unique selling proposition and selling scripts.

Simply download the form at *www.optimizeinc.net/ downloads* and break out into groups. Have each participant circle or dot the applicable terms that illustrate how your company delivers value. Based on the outcome of the exercise, your team can create a series of value statements.

For illustration, below is a value proposition statement created for one of our clients. Convaid, based in Torrance, California, manufactures pediatric wheelchairs. It provides a wide range of chairs to fulfill various consumer needs, including chairs for children with chronic diseases like cerebral palsy and muscular dystrophy. We use Convaid in our business case because the company sells a consumable product, but their relationship with dealers is B2B. Their value could be framed by:

- Expansive product line and strong product development engine. (Variety)
- As chairs are pre-assembled but made to order, the company's lead time is relatively short. (Saves Time)
- The company has exacting quality standards and is classified for reimbursement by Medicare. (Makes us Compliant/Quality)
- The company is a leader in consumer education. (Informs)
- The brand has many raving fans among occupational therapists, who might refer product placements to dealers. (Affiliation)
- Convaid products are well regarded because of their design and quality, and repeat business is high. (Customer Loyalty)

Having a differentiated value proposition is difficult in B2B, because the general construct of a value proposition is so similar from one company to the next.

For example, if you sell aerospace parts to original equipment manufacturers, the buying decision would focus on quality, delivery time and price. It is hard to win on unique capabilities because almost any competitor could buy the same equipment and hire similar people. Oftentimes, professional procurement organizations will select a vendor based on its performance against a scorecard. Professional procurement is designed to take differentiation, personal relationships and subjectivity out of the equation. Professional procurement professionals attempt to bake out all the other variables until they get to time, quality and price.

But digging deeper into client needs does provide an opportunity to unearth new information about the motives of buyers and how vendors can capitalize on nuances in their messaging and language. As we have defined it in the B2B Value Pyramid, multiple dimensions define why a customer buys. (Note that the value proposition for a B2C business would be very similar.) Customers buy based on these attributes and their need at a given time:

Functional Value. When they want a supplier who can "get the job done," that is, the cheapest alternative.

Technical Value. When they need information or access to highly specialized skills such as those provided by an architect, engineer or accountant. In manufacturing, they are the suppliers that provide better quality, design or processes. There is an implied brand value.

Emotional Value. When they want to have a connection with the people they work with or when a vendor enriches their lives beyond the business relationship. These suppliers provide brand intangibles such as recognition by peers.

Enterprise Value. When the vendor relationship is transformational enough that partnership with it increases the value of the company.

> ⚬ *A value proposition is most meaningful when a vendor can provide multiple value elements across several dimensions. The higher the element in the triangle, the higher its perceived value.*

Each company can create its own canvas to isolate the elements in its value proposition.

In another example, the aerospace supplier:

- Has the best quality available and rarely has a defect. The buyer will not be embarrassed. (Quality and safety)
- Integrates with its customers' systems. (Integration)
- Is fully compliant with FAA and other standards. (Makes us compliant)
- Agrees to sell ten parts to only that customer. (Exclusivity)
- Regularly invites the buyer to industry events. (Affiliation)
- Takes the client to baseball games or provides articles about the client's favorite team. (Affinity)

In this example, and in most all cases, price is a consideration, but it is not the most important purchase trigger. Providers achieve a tie with variables such as quality. Customers will find a handful of potential suppliers in a particular price range and select the one that meets their other criteria.

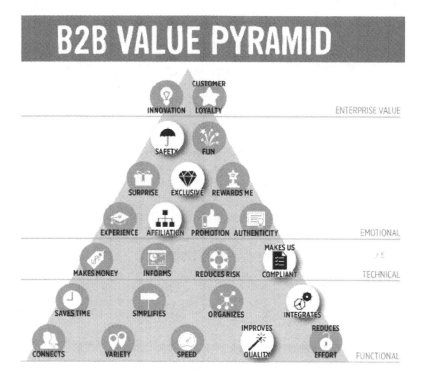

After the analysis is completed and a final pool determined, customers select the vendor they like. Numerous studies point out that even in professional procurement situations, companies within 5 percent of the lowest prices are often selected, proving that price is not the only consideration.

Yet consider our natural human buying behavior. There are some services we will naturally "trade up" for. Buyers will split nickels for workers' comp or janitorial services, but will pay $750 an hour for an intellectual property attorney. Technical skills carry value.

One might argue that functional or technical attributes are the most fundamental reasons why customers buy. But I would suggest that most of these attributes are merely the cost of admission. Customer loyalty, or "stickiness," is achieved when emotional connections are made, as well as when suppliers increase the value of their customers' businesses.

Customer loyalty is at the top of the pyramid (the most valuable). As an example, our firm uses market research to give our client projects more meaning. Thus, our market research partners are invaluable to us, because they increase our ability to obtain and keep clients.

Many people over the years have argued that professional buyers are trained to remove all emotion from the buying decision. However, their top priority is their own self-preservation. They simply don't want to make a mistake. If a manufacturing partner fails to ship on time or to spec, its reputation suffers. Therefore their buying decision is principally based on a balance of cost and "safety."

VALUE DRIVER:
UNIQUE VALUE PROPOSITION AND BRANDING THAT PROVES VALUE

Value Driver Tip—Companies must identify
at least three unique points of difference.
Branding (and all sales and marketing activities)
should reinforce these differences and
PROVE their value.

We have a manufacturing client that reinforces this paradigm. S&H Machine is an aerospace and defense machining operation in Burbank, California. Like many machining businesses, it is second-generation. David Fisher took over the business from his father in 2008. David is adept at navigating the difficult professional procurement environment. Companies in this space must deliver functional and technical value, both of which are reinforced with trust.

One day a professional buyer from a large aerospace concern showed up unannounced and asked to see David. The buyer explained that he wanted to tour the plant.

At one point during the tour, the buyer said he had seen performance statistics on the company's website. He asked David if those numbers truly reflected the real-time pulse of the S&H service level.

David took him to a monitor within the plant that provided employees with real-time performance metrics. He then pulled

down the numbers that proved the company's lead time, quality and on-time delivery statistics. The prospect was converted, and today, is one of S&H's largest customers.

In addition to performance statistics, S&H lists the top purchasing triggers on its website. You will find verbiage detailing why the company is great at performing against these triggers. David is deliberate about the language used to describe these purchase triggers, including "Competitive Pricing." Listing these purchase triggers implies that S&H will achieve a tie in of variables, such as pricing, and will win through better performance.

Thus, even in a professional procurement environment (and certainly in others), a supplier's ability to instill confidence is vital to its ability to acquire and keep clients. In this case, "safety" would be the emotional trigger a marketer would exploit. White papers could demonstrate innovation in the supply chain and methods used to ensure that performance metrics are satisfied. All sales and marketing activities should be in alignment with this value proposition (a combination of functional, technical and emotional value).

Numerous neuromarketing studies have revealed that more than 90 percent of purchase decisions are made subconsciously.[12]

To reap the maximum benefits from the B2B Value Pyramid, management teams should:

- Conduct significant research with customers on why they buy. This may be best achieved by having a neutral third party conduct interviews with current and past customers. Customers who made a recent buying decision may be the best source of information.

- Conduct a value pyramid exercise with their sales and marketing team. In an interactive setting, conduct a forced prioritization using sticky dots to select the most important attributes.
- Articulate their value proposition in a series of statements, as we have done above, that clarify how they deliver unique value.
- Conduct a sales and marketing summit, and develop an action plan of activities that rally sales and marketing teams around the value proposition.
- Ensure that all marketing collateral, digital assets and sales scripts support the value proposition.
- Employ the B2B Value Pyramid as a framework for identifying unique value and the full range of sales and marketing activities required to deliver it.

CHAPTER REVIEW

▸ One thing about the race to the bottom is that everybody loses.

▸ Entire industries create a cadence of competition. The more crowded a market, the more difficult it is to point out a brand's unique characteristics. Competitive herding is a consequence of entire industries taking on a cadence of competition.

▸ Industries are not commoditized; non-differentiated brands and products are.

▸ If a management team can't figure out how to be unique, the rest of its strategy is meaningless (unless it is positioned as the low-cost leader). If a company can't attract a premium for its product and is under constant price pressure, it is incumbent on the management team to act.

▸ Having a differentiated value proposition is very difficult in B2B, because the general construct of a value proposition is so similar from one company to the next.

▸ Pricing is a function of circumstances and usage.

▸ Your team can utilize the B2B Value Pyramid to build consensus on what attributes should be represented in your competencies, branding, unique selling proposition and selling scripts.

▸ Companies must identify at least three unique points of difference. Branding, and all sales and marketing activities, should reinforce these differences and PROVE their value.

Tools Offered in this Chapter:

B2B Value Pyramid Worksheet
www.optimizeinc.net/downloads

Chapter 4
INNOVATION IN AN AGE OF UNCERTAINTY

"If you change the way you look at your circumstances, your circumstances will change."

—Darren Hardy

YOU COULD DIVIDE OUR ECONOMY into two types of companies. There are Old World companies in industries that are slow to change. There is little innovation because these industries are mature. Then there are contemporary companies that are more agile because of the pace of change in the environment surrounding them.

There are two reasons Old World companies struggle with innovation. First is the common perception that innovation is a function of having innovative people. Such companies may employ some very creative people, but they may not have a structure that promotes innovation. Second, they may not have a culture of inclusion where innovation can bubble to the top.

In July 2013, Asiana Airlines flight 214 crashed into the seawall just short of the runway at San Francisco International Airport (SFO) with 291 passengers on board.[13] Three Chinese teenagers were killed and 187 people were injured, in the only fatal commercial flight in the United States in a five-year span.

It was pilot Lee Gang-guk's first time landing a Boeing 777 at SFO. Little did he know that one of his fellow pilots had unintentionally deactivated a system that automatically regulates air speed. The plane descended too quickly, was too low, and its landing speed was too slow.

When testifying at the National Transportation Safety Board hearing after the crash, Gang-guk tried to explain his reluctance to "initiate an emergency go-around" even though it had become obvious to him that the plane was in serious trouble. He said he did not want to acknowledge weakness and believed that only the instructor pilot "had the authority to initiate the maneuver."[14]

In the wake of the divesting crash, news channels were flooded with analysts who explained that within the Korean culture, junior pilots do not question senior pilots. A veteran pilot on a major international airline was willing to risk the lives of over 300 people, including his own, out of fear of questioning the decisions of people more senior to him.

Our unwillingness to question authority is human nature and universal across all cultures; imagine how midlevel managers feel in a typical company. Even under the best of circumstances, when senior managers are well intentioned about feedback, the opinions of employees are often not heard. At the very least they are muted in complex management structures that preserve the status quo. It is typical of senior managers to keep their business strategy close to the vest.

> *Strong leaders encourage dissent. They seek it out and reward it.*

Of course, some people constantly offer dissent because they are miserable people who are unhappy about everything. These are the people who are not fun to be around.

But there are others who are masterful at pointing out the flaw in a solution without attacking others. These are the provocative thinkers who are valuable to an organization. They ask why, and then they ask why again, in a way that makes others defend their decisions for the good of the company.

In most companies there are sacred cows. Some elements of strategy that could make or break a company are never discussed. For example, it would be taboo in many companies to discuss outsourcing (offshoring). Many of our clients are in California, where it is becoming more and more expensive to operate. Yet these conversations rarely occur in environments (such as in the case of a California employer that might consider a move) where competitive advantage may be at stake.

> *In other instances, entire skills sets critical to the success of a business are missing, and senior managers don't want to expose their weaknesses. These are conversations people simply do*

> *not want to have. It is critical in the formation of*
> *strategy that people put their cards on the table.*
> *True innovation requires touching the third rail*
> *and drilling down to the core of how a business*
> *delivers value.*

Much like flying an airplane, running a business today does not offer much time for critical conversations.

To think in disruptive, transformational terms is challenging for most businesspeople. When we extend this concept across an enterprise it is even harder. You may remember the study we cited in Chapter 1 that illustrated that only about 2 percent of firms can manage their core business well while they transform into new ones (for example, by adding new products).

As we identified, companies are not structured or well tooled to innovate. True innovation, by its very nature, is the exception and not the rule.

> *For this reason, innovators often need to be decoupled from the core business they are attempting to replace.*

Before even trying to innovate, develop new products or disrupt, those in management should ask themselves:

- Does our team today include disruptive thinkers?
- Do we seek out input from external stakeholders?
- Does our working environment promote innovation?

- Do we have dedicated resources (in the form of people) who have the time to innovate?
- When we recruit new people, is creativity an attribute we covet?
- What does our innovation portfolio look like today? What percent of our growth is expected to be core, versus non-core (adjacent and disruptive)?
- Do we celebrate failure and encourage dissent?
- Are we willing to have uncomfortable conversations that challenge underlying assumptions about our products?

As Nathan Furr and Jeff Dyer point out in their book, *The Innovator's Method*, there are at least three types of uncertainty that can be a catalyst to innovation.[15]

- **Demand Uncertainty.** Takes place when we are unsure if customers will buy a product or service.

- **Technology Uncertainty.** Occurs when the optimal method for providing the right solution has not been developed for the market.

- **Unknown Unknowns.** When latent customer needs have not yet been identified.

To wrestle with uncertainty, organizations must build systems that welcome and foster innovation. First, managers must encourage diversity of thought by regularly talking to a broad group of constituents and asking questions such as: "If you were me, what would you be thinking about?" Managers must be equipped to listen before they speak and welcome uncomfortable conversations with employees. They should also encourage risk taking, through non-monetary rewards. Charles Schwab holds a business conference each year in San Francisco, and invites employees who have submitted valued innovation ideas in the prior year.[16]

The greater the uncertainty in an industry, the greater investment required for innovation. Consider the research and development budgets estimated by PricewaterhouseCoopers for the top 1000 North American companies.[17]

Top % of Revenue	Total Investment (%)	($)
Software	14%	$60 Billion
Healthcare	10%	$70 Billion
Computing and Electronics	10%	$77 Billion
Bottom % of Revenue		
Telecom	1%	$2 Billion
Chemicals and Energy	2%	$11 Billion

Source: North America R&D Spending by top 1000 companies PWC

So innovation is more a function of industry and operating environment than it is of the attributes of a company's employees. Of course, within any sector there can be extremely creative companies that are likely to be disruptive.

Product development companies follow a disciplined process for building new products. Companies can model their own product development roadmap, but it should be a written-process flow document that is followed meticulously. Even as agile companies pivot on the fly, some processes need to be adhered to.

Here are steps you can follow in a product development process:

Identification. In this early stage, the inventor gets close to the customer and identifies stated or latent needs. The product development team creates a series of assumptions that will be the basis for developing features and benefits.

Information should be gathered from a broad range of constituents: customers, potential customers, suppliers, industry experts, employees, distributors and others.

Service companies attempting to identify how to extend their businesses should conduct a value chain analysis at this stage.

Problem Solving. Once needs have been identified, the team looks at many solutions and ultimately combines ideas from various visions of a product.

Experimentation. At this stage, test various prototypes to determine what works and what doesn't.

Market Evaluation. Parallel to the process of developing the product, marketing attempts to identify niches where a company can succeed.

Business Model Innovation. This is one of the most important yet most overlooked stages. Companies spend a lot of time developing products or core services and don't spend enough time thinking about the model they wrap around it. Every nuance, from delivery to pricing, is an opportunity to differentiate.

Minimally Viable Product. Specs for a product that could gain market acceptance are developed. It is also critical that the final positioning be considered so that the appropriate features may be added at a later date, but at the desired price point. Under these circumstances, "minimally viable" may not be enough.

Launch. During this phase, new distributors, dealers and users are trained to use the product or service. Often in this phase, companies are so focused on distribution that they fail to create a feedback loop to gain insight from early adopters.

Evaluation. It is critical that new products are evaluated in real time. Marketers should gather both demographic and psychographic information to confirm their initial assumptions.

As we have already discussed, companies can grow in two ways: vertically or horizontally. When they enter an adjacent market space, say a new geographic area, they are growing horizontally. When they re-engineer their business model to include participation in a broader portion of the value chain, they are taking part in "vertical integration."

A value chain is the sequence of activities a provider performs in delivering products or services.[18] *Value chain analysis breaks down the activities of a firm into its basic elements such as R&D, product development, marketing, and so forth.*

The value of these activities, as perceived by customers, is then weighed against the ability of the company and its competitors to deliver them. By completing a value chain analysis, the provider identifies:

- The product/service features and benefits customers value most
- New service bundles that can create differentiation
- The sweet spot for value proposition and marketing messaging

Michael Porter, the grandfather of business strategy, introduced the value chain in 1985. Porter characterized the steps in the chain as direct and indirect.

The key to a useful value chain analysis is to think of each segment as a value-creating activity, instead of as a cost.

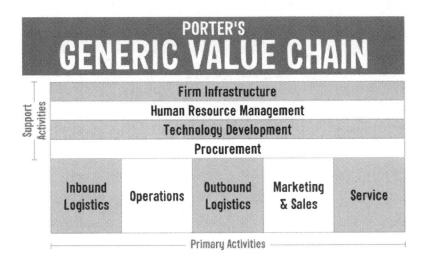

Let's look at the value chain of a business we all know—and one I have worked with and have insight into—Starbucks.

Inbound Logistics. Starbucks procures its own beans from select vendors in Latin America, Africa and Asia. Starbucks hand selects varieties for specific coffee blends. It self-distributes the bulk of supplies to its stores.

Operations. Starbucks operates its own stores worldwide, including the U.S. Starbucks is a gathering place for people wishing to meet.

Outbound Logistics. Starbucks licenses a few products, but for the most part there is little in the way of outbound logistics, since its core product is contained in its retail operations.

Marketing and Sales. Until recently Starbucks has not participated in traditional advertising. The company's marketing has been word-of-mouth.

Service. Starbucks maintains strong loyalty and raving fans because of its fanatical approach to service and inviting amenities. The company has expanded the use of technology in its stores for online ordering and the like.

If a strategist were considering service expansion for Starbucks, he or she might evaluate relative value for consumers in stores as:

	Starbucks	Competitor	Value Rank
R&D-New Products	.60	.40	3
Menu Development	.60	.20	3
Procurement	.30	.50	4
Inbound logistics	.20	.20	5
Service	.75	.60	2
Environment and Meeting Place	.90	.60	1
Outbound Logistics	.10	.75	6
Cost of a Cappuccino	$3.25	$3.25	

In this case, the greatest perceived value is captured within the store environment and through the service provided by staff. The strategist may compare Starbucks with a local coffee establishment that does not procure direct and does not have an ever-changing, dynamic menu.

Using the logic of the value chain, Starbucks might consider the services directly above and below its sweet spot in terms of valued services.

For example, Starbucks might consider delivery, which would extend perceived value from its environment into outbound logistics. Charles Schwab disrupted the market for stockbrokers by altering the accepted value proposition. It's not that Schwab offered different benefits; it's that it magnified the significance of some features over others.[19]

Although investors may value advice, Schwab customers gravitated to a low-cost alternative that redefined the cost-benefit of executing a trade. These customers offered a sizable enough market for Schwab to carve out a sustainable business. Conversely, Schwab also identified a benefit—advice—that was overserved in the market and de-emphasized its importance. This is exactly how commoditization comes to be.

A value chain analysis makes a distinction between delivering the most value, and measuring relative cost vs. relative value. Customers may value warranties as a differentiator among companies. Some competitors, like BMW or Hyundai, may excel in delivering such a benefit, which may offer some advantage. What is critical is that the providers measure the perceived value of the feature vs. the incremental cost to provide it. Many companies use warranties in this way because as a percentage of revenue, the cost of warranties is very low.

An additional benefit of a value chain analysis is that it forces the marketer to look beyond existing capabilities as well as to evaluate them against those offered by others, vis-à-vis customer needs.

VALUE DRIVER:
BUSINESS MODEL & SUSTAINABLE REVENUE MODEL

Value Driver Tip—Use value chain analysis to understand your company's role in the value chain, and identify features or services adjacent to those you're already in.

Here is a step-by-step guide for conducting a value chain analysis. The example below is for a fictitious company producing vitamin supplements:

STEP 1. IDENTIFY THE ACTIVITIES OF THE VALUE CHAIN.

Break down each component of your product into activities within its life cycle. Do not list support functions such as HR that don't directly contribute to the value perceived by clients.

STEP 2. ASSIGN A TRUE COST TO EACH ACTIVITY.

Quantify the costs associated with each step in the value chain. Ideally, this would include a specific accounting of labor costs associated with production or delivery of a service, down to a per-unit basis. Often, companies employ an activity based costing technique to gather such information, which may require hiring a consulting or accounting firm.

STEP 3. MEASURE THE RELATIVE VALUE OF EACH SEGMENT.

Perhaps the most difficult element within value chain analysis is gauging the benefits that customers or clients value most. Unlike the other steps, this requires information external to the organization. This is typically accomplished through a customer insight study, customer survey, customer advisory board or a focus group. Asking customers what they value, including benefits offered by competitors, may be intimidating, but it is absolutely necessary. An emerging tool is online panels that gather opinions of potential customers at low cost.

STEP 4. WEIGH STRENGTHS AND WEAKNESSES OF COMPETITORS FOR EACH ACTIVITY.

Evaluate your organization's ability to deliver unique value in each activity and compare that with the capabilities of your competitors.

In the example below:

- Each value-based activity is listed
- A total direct cost is calculated and assigned
- The ability of the company to provide unique value is articulated by a + or – (strength or weakness)
- The ability of competitors to provide unique value is articulated by a + or – (strength or weakness)
- The value of each activity (as perceived by customers) is ranked

To download the Value Chain White Paper: *www.optimizeinc.net/downloads*

Here is another example, in a slightly different format, for a B2B chemical company.

Activity	Value $	Client	Comp A	Value Rank
R & D	$2.50	–	+	
Formulation	$2.75		–	1
Testing	$1.00		–	
Marketing	$4.00	+		
Customer Service	$4.50		+	
Production	$6.00		+	2
Shipping	$3.00	+		
Invoicing	$0.50			
Confirmation	$0.25			3

The data reveals that the most important feature to customers is the custom formulation produced for them.

Although factors such as product quality, packaging and cycle time may be intuitive benefits that may be the focus of manufacturers, they are not the features that produce the greatest relative value vs. relative cost.

In fact, the greatest "value add" for the provider may be in the confirmation (at virtually no cost), which delivers greater benefit in relative terms than the production of the product itself. See Chapter 2 for a list of features and services that are on the "edge of the offer."

This analysis can be the foundation for many important management decisions. For example, the decision to outsource production or customer service should not be made based on cost savings, but on relative value delivered to a customer.

In this example, customers value the customer service agent more than fast cycle time, and an argument could be made to outsource production and keep customer service in-house.

Thus, value chain analysis is an immensely powerful tool in identifying how to deliver unique value, and to create an infrastructure that supports it.

QUESTIONS TO ASK/ASSUMPTIONS TO CHALLENGE:

As your team begins to identify a product/service offering, it should ask the following questions.[20]

- What is the growth of the market?
- What technology do we expect to emerge? How quickly is it likely to be adopted?
- What price points would change behavior?
- What new competition could enter the space?
- Would the competition be likely to focus on our model, or a different one?
- Which customers are under-served? Which are over-served?

If you would like to conduct an innovation exercise with your team, download the Business Innovation Tool at: *www.optimizeinc.net/downloads*

BUSINESS MODEL INNOVATION

Once a value chain exercise has been completed, a company can consider if tweaking or re-engineering its business model could inspire framing a new value proposition. The following are business model types to consider.

Models that define new applications of existing products.

History is riddled with technologies that have been repackaged for new uses. The most stimulating—sorry, I couldn't help myself—is Viagra.[21] It was first developed as a medication for heart disease. Though it turned out to be ineffective as a heart medication, researchers did find a notable side effect, if you catch my drift.

Models that deliver more value to customers.

These models include methods for proving that a supplier delivers incremental benefits. Trunk Club provides consumers with a customized wardrobe, shipped automatically. Others may provide superior product performance. Attributes of this model type include:

- Integration platforms
- Mass customization

Models that reduce client's total cost of ownership.

These models (such as insurance) protect clients from risks. Attributes include:

- Usage pricing
- Auctions

- Fixed price
- "Just good enough" quality
- Self-service

Models that grow the size of the market.

These models are demand-based. For example, franchising provides instant scalability because franchisors do not need to employ management staff, hourly workers or long-term real estate commitments. Attributes include:

- Ecommerce/web
- Franchising
- Licensing
- Co-branding
- Long Tail (reverse of Pareto principle)
- Freemium (upgrading from free)

Models that deepen customer relationships.

In many manufacturing environments including aerospace, supplier and customer will enter longer term agreements so the supplier can buy specialized equipment with the express purpose of fulfilling customer needs. Software has moved to Software as a Service, or SaaS. Attributes include:

- Long-term agreements
- Subscription pricing

Models that establish a network or platform.

Networks are "two-sided": they create a network for buyer and seller. Platforms are integrated systems that tie together a business and its data, and promote many profit centers. Examples include eBay, Amazon and Uber. Attributes include:

- Crowdsourcing
- Crowdfunding
- Multiple-sided platform
- Open-source

Models that produce a finance arbitrage.

Some businesses make money off financial "float," or by leveraging outside capabilities. Made popular in the book *The 4-Hour Workweek*, these businesses are almost entirely outsourced. Attributes include:

- Negative Cash Operating Cycle (get paid before paying for raw materials and labor)

Radical Pricing Models.

In these businesses, the monetization method is unique. Attributes include:

- Barter
- Fractional and pay-as-you-go (time share, Zipcar)
- Skin in the game (based on performance incentives)
- Razor and blade (give away the razor and sell the blades)
- Super-premium

Models that tinker with the bundle of services.

These companies leverage the value chain very well and extend the service bundle. Attributes include:

- Cross-selling model
- One-stop shopping (solutions)
- Catalog

Models that provide access to information.
These models leverage their superior analytics capability to sell information that is often more valuable than the core business from which the information comes. Attributes include:

- "Big Data" play
- Reporting

Reverse Business Models.
These businesses are the opposite of a platform.[22] Tech companies, especially, have been removing features to provide services that are just good enough. Attributes include:

- Minimally acceptable products
- Convenience products

THE THREE STAGES OF INNOVATION

There are also industry life cycle stages where the following types of innovation are prevalent:

- Market Disruption
- Up-Market Disruption
- Low-End Disruption

Although both incumbents and entrants may have the same opportunities within a market, their behavior within it will vary greatly, based on their motivation. Here's a universal truth about new competition: It is most often offered by new entrants that compete on price, since no special capabilities are required to do so, and they have heightened motivation to sell at a loss.

Over time, companies improve their technology and processes and thus perform at a higher level (known as the experience curve). Absent of better quality gained through the experience curve or channel advantage, or other levers discussed in this book, companies nip at incumbents' heels.

The more established the incumbent, the more its systems and processes are rooted in best practices; they have a methodical, prodding approach to new products and services. I'm not suggesting that mere size makes a company inefficient or unable to innovate; I'm suggesting that new entrants in a market are motivated to take bigger risks. The other characteristic of entrants is the likelihood that they will initially specialize in a sector based on their limited expertise and capital constraints.

Consider men's active wear. Through the '70s and '80s, the leading U.S. brands were Converse and Adidas. In the '90s, Nike burst onto the scene as the innovator. Nike initially sold footwear—especially basketball shoes—ultimately expanding into a myriad of apparel, shoes and sporting goods from tennis to golf. Then came Nike's series of high-profile celebrity endorsement signings including those by Michael Jordan and Tiger Woods. By 2005, Nike had achieved sales of $13 billion.

Nike didn't pay much attention to a new entrant: Under Armour. The company was started by a University of Maryland football player, Kevin Plank, out of his grandmother's garage.[23]

Plank identified a blended moisture wicker material that he turned into an undergarment for football players. The brand gained a modest following with less than $100,000 in sales in 1997.

When Oakland Raiders quarterback Jeff George was seen wearing an Under Armour mock in a photograph in *USA Today*, a Georgia Tech equipment manager ordered 350 pieces. At the time, it was the company's only significant order from a customer of any consequence. In its initial growth stage, the company gained penetration with professional athletes, and the brand took off.

The company ran ads that were edgy and high-adrenaline, with menacing football players grunting and growling, using aggressive messaging like "Protect the House." The brand came off as highly authentic and rugged. It took on a mystique. As Under Armour gained distribution and awareness, it spread to new sports segments, including baseball, tennis and golf.

Ironically, Nike was an entrant that had become an incumbent, then did a poor job fending off a new competitor. The entrant dominated a relatively small, unrealized and specialized market—undergarments. Nike evidently did not see this piece of the market warranting investment (defense).

Nike's priorities and willingness to innovate or even copy were driven by the company's resources and motivation.

An entrant into a "white space" must take unmitigated risk. Market data is available only for existing businesses, so such innovation is a bet that new features or benefits will improve the experience of buyers in a material way.

A new entrant that creates a market in a white space has the largest upside for expediential growth. The entrant is competing against non-competition and thus can command high margins, as in the case of Square (the merchant services firm). This window of opportunity closes quickly, and the innovator has a finite amount of time to position itself as the market leader.

If innovation were plotted on a continuum, new market entrants would be the most disruptive; incumbents would be the least. Although start-ups or entrants are driven by growth, incumbents are driven by self-preservation. One is playing offense; the other, defense.

The incumbent possesses characteristics that enable it to defend its position. For example, Nike's foothold on distribution could have presented an obstacle for Under Armour, since professional buyers may have been limited to purchasing more established brands.

Ironically, these same characteristics can work against the incumbent. Nike's existing distribution relationships may have restricted innovation. A desire to limit inventory may have provided a disincentive to take a big risk, such as expanding into undergarments.

Identifying a company's market can be influenced by its experience. A company may be inclined to more deeply penetrate its core market, rather than be committed to trade up or down to win new clients.

> ☼ *This first phase of innovation is known as Market Disruption.*

When a market is nearing maturity, but is not yet saturated, entrants may attempt to provide new features or benefits that improve the utility of its products or services. A classic example is the shift to on-demand content. Famously, Netflix founder Reed Hastings approached Blockbuster CEO John Antioco in 2000 and offered to sell him the company for $50 million.

Antioco passed, saying he perceived Netflix as a "very small niche business."[24] Blockbuster ceased operations in 2013. In 2016, online movie subscription services, including Netflix, had a 59 percent share of U.S. movie revenue.[25]

What's interesting about the rise of Netflix and streaming video is that the core product didn't change; the delivery system did. Movies have evolved but their nature is essentially unchanged.

What did change was a shift from physical movies and stores to digital downloads with a radically different pricing model. (Blockbuster made its money on late fees.) The infrastructure required to support the legacy model was far costlier than the digital model. Product innovation did not win out; service model innovation did.

But business model innovation would not have been as relevant if movies had not already been positioned as a viable product. Renting a movie at Blockbuster was an alternative to the theatre; then Netflix became an alternative to Blockbuster. If not for video rental stores, digital downloads may not have been possible, or at least their adoption would have taken place at a slower rate.

> We refer to this second phase as Up-Market Disruption—when material improvements are made to how products are produced, delivered or used.

The term "disruptive technology" was first introduced by Clayton Christensen in his revolutionary book, *The Innovator's Dilemma*. Since the book's release in 1997, many have misused the term disruptive innovation, which is often used to describe any radically transformative business model. But that is not the proper application of Christensen's theory.

Disruptive technology describes technologies that scale existing product categories, generally at lower cost. Square, Uber or Samsung's entry level virtual reality products may qualify as true disruptive technologies, which fall within what we would describe as Phase 3 Innovations.

Yet Phase 3 Innovations may include products or services that do not offer a leap in terms of new utility. Larger, well established companies will invest more heavily in supporting the status quo, but make subtle changes in terms of utility or usefulness.

When McDonald's, to combat Starbucks, began offering its McCafé coffee line, it did not offer new varieties of coffees. The expansion of its menu merely supported the status quo, because McDonald's enjoys such massive scale that a duel with Starbucks based on sameness played to its strategic advantage. McDonald's lacked motivation to offer a "leap of innovation."

When a market is crowded, innovation is geared toward efficiency and cost reduction. When Southwest Airlines entered the airline industry, the air travel market was oversaturated with a glut of providers that looked and acted the same—American, Continental, Delta and United, to name a few.

Thus, Southwest's innovations toward standardized aircraft, the elimination of services like food, and its hub-and-spoke distribution system were all geared toward the lowest price offer.

Focus on scale and efficiencies within a mature market is defined as Low-End Disruption.

We have presented you with three types of innovations:

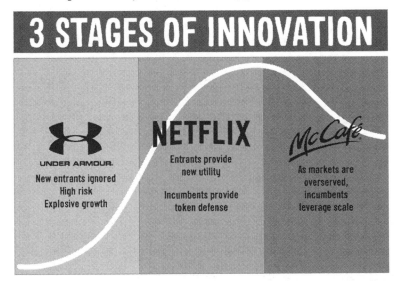

Phase 1: Market Disruption (Introduction). When a market does not exist, and an entrant "makes" the market, such as with Under Armour.

Phase 2: Up-Market Disruption (Adoption). When a market exists but has not reached maturity, and an entrant, like Netflix, innovates to improve utility.

Phase 3: Low-End Disruption (Scale). When a market is mature and an incumbent utilizes its leverage and scale to commoditize it, as with McCafé.

> *The innovator, seeking out a differentiator that will ignite its business and create separation, must consider the cycle of any industry it wishes to enter and the resource constraints that might hinder expansion.*

The phases within a company's life cycle are of equal importance. When Under Armour was in its introductory phase, it would not have had the manufacturing resources or technical prowess to sell product to a Dick's Sporting Goods or other national chain.

In its adoption phase it may have been able to dramatically expand its production capability within a limited offering, but may not have had the capital to fund expansion into new product categories.

Finally, the innovator must consider the economic cycle. In the case of physical goods like sports apparel, retailers cut inventories when the economy is weak, and expand product lines and store counts when the economy is growing. The market may be more accepting of innovations that cut costs in a down economic cycle.

CHAPTER REVIEW

- ▸ Strong leaders encourage dissent. They seek it out and reward it.

- ▸ There are conversations people simply do not want to have. It is critical in the formation of strategy that all the cards be placed on the table.

- ▸ A value chain is the sequence of activities a provider performs in delivering products or services. Value chain analysis breaks down the activities of a firm into its basic elements: R&D, product development, marketing and more.

- ▸ The key to a useful value chain analysis is to think of each segment as a value-creating activity instead of as a cost.

- ▸ Innovators often need to be decoupled from the core business they are trying to replace.

- ▸ There are three phases within innovation:
  - ○ Market disruption
  - ○ Up-Market disruption
  - ○ Low-End disruption

- ▸ The innovator, seeking out a differentiator to ignite its business and create separation, must consider the cycle of any industry it wishes to enter, and the resource constraints that might hinder expansion.

- ► Companies must constantly reevaluate their business models and create sustainable revenue models. It is likely that business model innovation will occur after the product acceptance phase.

Tools Offered in this Chapter:

Value Chain White Paper
www.optimizeinc.net/downloads

Business Model Innovation Tool
www.optimizeinc.net/downloads

Chapter 5
ENVIRONMENTAL SCAN—THE FORCES AROUND US

"This is the future—and everything else is going to look obsolete, like sending messages with pigeons."
—Carlos Ghosn, former Nissan CEO

WROTE MY FIRST BOOK, *Intended Consequences*, in 2009. It reflected my personal beliefs. On the heels of the liquidity crisis, I had met business owners who acted as if they had lost all hope, given the market conditions in their industries. The successful entrepreneur within a sustainable business designs the future he or she wants to create. The entrepreneur is not a victim of circumstance; he takes advantage of circumstance. Great entrepreneurs are market-focused, and they are strategic most of the time.

As Stephen Covey proclaimed, we must first seek to understand and then to be understood. In the quest for understanding, the strategist starts with a broad understanding of long-term environmental trends that could impact demand.

I often ask to see C-level executives' strategic plans. They send me a spreadsheet with revenue and EBITDA numbers. Or they talk about their competitors and customers. As we will discuss shortly, a thoughtful strategic plan includes the evaluation of external elements and does this before a market analysis is performed.

> 💡 *Such external impacts could be organized into five sections: Social, Technological, Economic, Ecological and Political. To better understand these trends, we would typically conduct a STEEP Analysis—a framework to gauge how external factors will impact demand.*

We look for trends that could impact our industry in the next three to five years or longer. As of this writing, here are some long-term trends to consider:

From Megacities to Megaregions

Within the last 25 years, we have seen the proliferation of megacities (those with over 10 million residents).[26] Vast numbers of millennials are moving to suburbs to find quality of life. As infrastructure becomes strained, there will be cooperation across megaregions, which will promote mixed-use properties, networks, public transit, bike lanes, and so forth. City centers will be shopping and culture epicenters inhabited by "zero-children" households.

By 2020, we can expect to see 40 global smart cities, each identified by eight "smart" attributes: Governance, Energy, Building, Mobility, Infrastructure, Technology, Healthcare and Citizens. They'll include Seattle, Vancouver, London and Amsterdam, as energy, automation and IT companies converge to build infrastructure in these cities.

Shifts in Monetary Policy

The United States has entered a recession every six to seven years since the 1950s.[27] The Federal Reserve has responded by flooding the market with liquidity. In the future, mired in debt, the federal government will not have the ammunition with which to counter such cycles.

Electric Mobility

By 2020, global distribution of two- and four-wheel electric vehicles will exceed 40 million. These vehicles will come in new forms. Mopeds and Peapod vehicles (smart cars) will become ubiquitous in U.S. cities.

The spread of electric mobility will, in part, be precipitated by a network of charging stations provided by utilities, integrators, manufacturers and government.

Geo Tracking

Our cell phones will function like dating apps, tracking our movements and providing new opportunities to connect and engage. Digital marketing applications will provide pertinent offers, and we will gain new access to business opportunities based on our location.

Information Warfare

Over 1,000 satellites will be launched in the next decade. They will oversee GPS, communications and ballistic missile defenses. Computer code will be "weaponized" because data is the fuel of the digital age.[28]

Companies will be forced to protect themselves with cyber security, which is already a fundamental requirement of corporate governance. Fortunately, the United States still has a lead in cyber security, but China, Russia, Iran, the UK and Israel have significant capabilities.

Although cyber espionage from China remains a significant threat, the loss of intellectual property may be far more pervasive. It is estimated that China now steals $300 billion in IP (intellectual property) annually.[29]

The ransomware protection market is projected to be $17 billion by 2021.

Cybercrime is no longer just a nuisance. According to AT&T, 73 percent of surveyed American companies were victims of ransomware attacks in 2015.

With the proliferation of systems and devices—including hundreds of thousands of Internet of Things (IoT) devices—cybercriminals have more points of entry. Cyberattacks are only expected to increase. Security experts point out that adaptive security architecture is required to fend off multilayer attacks, including targeted espionage, ransomware, denial of service and privacy.

The adoption of new technology isn't slowing, either. In fact, disruptive technologies are accelerating in many sectors. As 5G (5th generation mobile networks) comes online by 2020, mobile processing speeds are expected to increase ten to 100 times, which will enable even faster computing.

Digital Mashup

The convergence of virtual reality, artificial intelligence and big data will erupt in the next five years. Virtual reality has the potential to impact B2B companies in many ways. Imagine a world where:

- Virtual reality training programs allow new employees to walk through a facility and practice safety techniques or receive on-the-job training through a device worn like a mask
- Remote operation of heavy equipment (such as excavators) expands access, lowers costs and improves safety
- 3D business meetings enable users to act and move as if they are in a physical meeting room
- Virtual storefronts allow consumers to try on clothes and garments, and custom-tailored garments are shipped on demand

- Remote healthcare allows surgeons to perform intricate, specialized surgeries from anywhere in the world

We are on the brink of a new frontier, one where systems can learn, adapt and think for themselves—as opposed to making decisions based on predesigned instructions.

The combination of greater processing power and more sophisticated algorithms will open up new possibilities. For example, consider how voice-activated virtual assistants—think Siri or Alexa on steroids—could help busy executives manage a variety of tasks. The assistant might, say, capture content an executive dictates to it and then edit and store it for others to consume. The continuity offered through this process is known as Ambient User Experience.

Technologies that are part of the IoT are also growing more "intelligent." They can collaborate with other devices, like Alexa, to command your music, air conditioning or security, based on what they "learn" about you.

The big data floodgates will open.

Faster processing speeds and relational databases will provide an environment where companies will finally realize the potential of big data. Driven by a need for deeper customer engagement, devices such as mobile, wearable and IoT will drive behavior and analytics.

Investing in technologies that improve efficiency or reduce cost is no longer good enough. As companies forge ahead, their integrated systems will permit them to compete more readily with larger companies and provide meaningful analytics that will enrich the customer experience.

Consider big data's utility in healthcare today. The Centers for Disease Control and Prevention uses big data to curb illness, and physicians use it for chronic disease management, by using technologies including wearables, healthcare robots, artificial intelligence and IoT. As these explode onto the scene, the healthcare IT infrastructure is being strained (electronic medical records are still only three to four years old). But within a few years, medical science will become better equipped to digest troves of patient data gathered from multiple fronts.

SMART ROBOTICS

To date, robots have been used primarily to replace remedial, repetitive tasks in manufacturing environments and the like.[30] But a confluence of recent technological advancements, including richly engineered software and faster processing speeds, offers something unprecedented. Today's robots are capable of spatial reasoning and situational awareness. In other words, they can think for themselves.[31] Although it may be an inconvenient truth, robots that can replace labor at $4 per hour will take on a bigger role in our economy. In Manila, more than 1.2 million call center jobs that were once high-end technology careers, such as network monitoring, are now done by robots.[32]

The next generation of robots will, for the first time, conduct tasks that were once reserved for surgeons and nurses, as well as other jobs that require human judgment.

Although some may be threatened by the expanse of computers, we should also recognize that they will undoubtedly have many benefits to society. New materials are making robots lighter and more compact. Nano-robots are smaller than a pebble and can perform medical procedures unmatched by doctors.

It is estimated that up to 50 percent of jobs in the U.S. could be replaced in the next two decades.[33] For example, restaurant workers are likely to be replaced by self-ordering, and even automated, food-to-go systems.

LABOR ON-DEMAND

Today's hypercompetitive marketplace demands high utilization of assets. A paradigm shift that is occurring rapidly is toward the full utilization of human capital.

The "gig economy" is on the rise. It's estimated that the economy today comprises over 60 million freelancers.[34] Independent contractors are expected to comprise 50 percent of the U.S. workforce by 2020. According to Deloitte, more than half of executives surveyed expected to increase their use of independent workers between now and then.

Clearly, our economy is moving toward non-traditional work environments. In the past contractors have been used for short-term projects. On-demand, first made popular by Uber, has also become popular in marketing, social media and administrative roles.

Work Intermediation Platforms (WIPs) are like freelancer management platforms that serve as a digital bridge between employers and workers.[35]

In the future, on-demand workers will fill pivotal roles that do not comprise full time positions. One survey revealed 59 percent of businesses use on-demand talent for projects that exceed six months.[36] With their diverse skill sets, these specialists are more productive than generalist office workers.

In part, technology is the impetus to this change. Powerful scheduling software and collaboration tools facilitate pairing up supply and demand.

Online platforms such as Freelancer and Upwork provide exchanges where freelancers offer their skills on an hourly basis.

On-demand labor is not without controversy. When Uber began, it was accused of robbing workers of protections including workers' compensation insurance, a minimum wage and discrimination protections.[37] But employers are beginning to see the value of treating their contractors like employees—and protecting themselves from costly litigation. In 2000, Microsoft paid $97 million to the Internal Revenue Service due to misclassification of employees.

Demographics are also driving the gig economy. As boomers retire they will look for fractional revenue to supplement their income.

DIGITAL BANKING

Traditional banks have had a moat built around them: distribution through branches, specialized expertise, hefty regulation and access to their deposits as a lifeline.

It wasn't too long ago that consumers did not trust mobile apps for banking. Today's high-quality web and mobile apps make banking seamless.[38]

The brick-and-mortar bank is reaching the end of its life cycle. In the future, apps will not only be used for tracking account activity, but will be the place where new accounts are opened and loan originations will occur. You can already fill out a new home loan application on a smart phone.

Digital banking is already in play in emerging economies where geography, violence and corruption provide significant barriers for banks and their customers. Digital currencies like Bitcoin are popular and their use will only proliferate as traditional consumers gain comfort with them.

HUMAN GENOME

As Alec Ross describes in his excellent book, *The Industries of the Future,* "The last trillion-dollar industry was built on a code of 1s and 0s. The next will be built on our genetic code."

The sequencing of the human genome was among the greatest accomplishments of the last decade. All cancers, and many similar conditions, begin with damaged DNA, and the human genome holds the key to the end of many diseases.

The promise of this work goes well beyond curing disease and toward "hacking" our bodies and unlocking our brains so that medical science can gain new understanding, which could completely transform medicine.

Along the way, more practical applications such as genetic testing available at your local grocery store, will dominate the news. Regulators will continue to monitor the use of tools (such as genetic testing) that have come under fire because of their inconsistency.

A more precise method will expand in the form of "risk engines" which mix physical, environmental and behavioral indicators to build a more precise model for health risks.

This is just a sampling of trends that will impact demand in many industries.

> *The master strategist examines these trends carefully through STEEP Analysis. To take such an exercise further, a management team can combine such trends in a scenario-planning exercise.*

Let's assume your company is in the construction sector, focused on government work.

Current Reality: Upcycle in construction yields 4 percent increase in demand.

Trends:

- Megaregions and Smart Cities
- Failing infrastructure in U.S. cities
- New administration that has promised to promote a jobs bill and to fix broken infrastructure

Implication: Construction companies will be positioning to leverage technology to create Smart Infrastructure. Such companies will thrive in megaregions and secondary cities like Austin, Texas and Denver, Colorado.

Scenario: Company creates Smart Infrastructure divisions as an adjacent business. It would be staffed with younger construction workers who understand technology. The company will partner with government agencies and other builders on large projects, funded by the federal government.

I would note that some executives think that scenario planning is some form of voodoo. I suggest that nothing in this plan is like reading a crystal ball. To the contrary, such scenarios are based on facts already in evidence today.

To conduct a STEEP Analysis, download the form at *www.optimizeinc.net/downloads*

CHAPTER REVIEW

- ▸ External factors can be organized into five sections: Social, Technological, Economic, Ecological and Political. To better understand these trends, strategists should conduct a STEEP Analysis.

- ▸ Strategists must examine these trends carefully. To take such an exercise further, a management team can combine these trends in a scenario-planning exercise.

- ▸ Examples of mega-trends to consider:
  - ○ From megacities to megaregions
  - ○ Shifts in monetary policy

- Electric mobility
- Geo tracking
- Information warfare
- Digital mashup
- Smart robots
- Labor on-demand
- Digital banking
- Human genome

Tools Offered in this Chapter:

STEEP Analysis Tool
www.optimizeinc.net/downloads

Chapter 6
THE KEYS TO THE CASTLE—BUSINESS INTELLIGENCE

"A wise man learns more from his enemies
than a fool from his friends."
—Baltasar Gracián

N THIS CHAPTER, WE WILL examine external and internal data points critical in the formation of strategy. The master strategist understands environmental and market trends external to the business, as well as the mechanics driving performance within it.

I was once working with a provider of corrugated cardboard and point-of-sale materials. The business had started to plateau, pricing was compressed and margins were eroding.

Traditional approaches to sales and marketing were only yielding lackluster results.

During strategic planning, I asked where and how the company, which had been successful in selling into the emerging electronics market, could grow. But management was having difficulty identifying what product categories and specific manufacturing companies would be a good fit for its products and services.

The company was based in Southern California, not far from the Port of Los Angeles. I suggested we try to learn what products were sold, in what volume, and shipped through the port. It turned out that information about the freight passing through the port is in the public record.

My team paid a fee to access such records and assembled a list of companies, products and volumes shipping through the port. The client now had a list of prospects, their ship volume and insight into which of its product applications might be most useful.

I asked my client if the information was helpful. I will never forget his response. He said we had given him "the keys to the castle."

In another instance, I was working with an industrial products provider, also based in California. Its sales and service system required "boots on the ground"—meaning geographic expansion would require investment in a local team. The sales team estimated market share to be 20 percent in Southern and Central California and much less in Northern California.

The executive team thought they should expand throughout the West into New Mexico, Colorado, Texas, Oregon and

Washington. We conducted a market study to estimate the size and corresponding growth rates of their target markets. It revealed that the California market was about the same size as all the other markets combined.

Further projections revealed that the company's customer acquisition cost would increase dramatically in the new markets. In other words, investment in the existing market offered a potentially higher ROI than expansion into new ones.

Companies have valuable internal data that is often untapped. One of our former clients (before a successful divesture in an industry roll-up) was one of the country's largest distributors to restaurants. In preparation for strategic planning, I asked that we segment the business, for example, by geography, category, and customer order size. We learned something astonishing: roughly 600 of its 3,000 customers were unprofitable.

During our strategic planning, the company decided to establish a delivery minimum, in alignment with selling "inside-out," which we will further discuss later in this chapter. This decision was the source of rigorous debate. Many sales team members felt strongly that the company would lose customers and potentially valuable referral sources. Their gut told them imposing a delivery minimum would be a big mistake.

In the following year's strategic planning, we ran the analysis again. About half the unprofitable customers had not ordered since the minimum was put in place. But the other half had actually bought much more than the year prior. The company's net margin went up an entire percentage point.

Doing the math provided more meaningful information than gut instincts did, and the decision materially improved profitability.

> *I am astonished at how often companies make strategic decisions with no data in the form of internal metrics or external market research. Often, managers will ignore information they view as inaccurate.*
>
> *Market research, such as that found in strategic planning, is imperfect. Yet some information is better than no information.*

Segmentation of a business is critical to understanding its underlying dynamics. Segmenting by channel, region, product category or customers is critical in making decisions about where to deploy resources: sales, marketing, engineering or production capabilities.

Marketers struggle with accessing information. And although market research databases are available for consultants like me to procure, for most clients such licenses would be prohibitive. But there are ways to gather information in advance of a strategic planning session, and, in fact, some information is not that hard to gather or access.

There are several data elements that are critical in almost every strategic plan:

- What is the company's existing growth rate?
- What is the industry size?
- What is the industry's growth rate?

- What is the size and growth rate of alternative industries we might enter?
- What is our market share or penetration in our existing segments?
- What is the contribution of each of our existing segments?

An analysis of segments may look like this:

	Revenue	Existing Market Potential	Penetration	Growth Rate	4 Yr Potential	Best-in-Class	Margin Potential	Target Penetration	Target Revenue
Drug Retailers	$4,500,000	$95,000,000	5%	2%	$102,600,000	Hi	Low	10%	$10,260,000
Other Retailers	$4,250,000	$125,000,000	3%	3%	$141,250,000	Low	Very Low	7%	$9,887,500
Nutrition Retailers	$4,200,000	$85,000,000	5%	2%	$91,800,000	Hi	High	7%	$6,426,000
Consumer Direct	$2,250,000	$100,000,000	2%	10%	$146,000,000	Hi	High	12%	$16,790,000
Others	$750,000	$15,000,000	5%	0%	$15,000,000	Low	Low	8%	$400,000
Totals	$15,950,000								$43,763,500

Management teams can evaluate their momentum through market share, penetration and total addressable market.

Market Share: The total percentage of volume sold by a supplier in a given market.

Penetration: The proportion of customers served in a market (even if they spend just one dollar with a supplier).

Total Addressable Market: The percentage of volume that can be expected within the target market. This metric may also recognize that customers routinely split volume across suppliers, and the maximum volume that can be achieved may represent a percentage of their purchases.

> *Research is either primary or secondary.*
> *Primary research is research conducted for the first time. It's typically designed to solve specific problems or gain new insight. Methods may include surveys, panels or interviews.*
> *Secondary research is conducted by accessing existing sources: online searches, white papers, academic research and more.*

Numerous free or low-cost resources can be used to develop market studies and the like. Some examples:

www.data.com—A lead-generation supplement to Salesforce

www.researchnow.com—Provides custom market research, including product-launch viability

www.moz.com—Provides quick website analytics for any site, including competitors' sites

www.gutcheckit.com—Provides consumer on-demand qualitative and quantitative agile market research

www.usertesting.com—Provides user insights to test websites and applications

www.bls.gov—Bureau of Labor Statistics

www.bea.gov—Bureau of Economic Analysis

Additional sources for business and market intelligence include:

INTERNAL SOURCES

- Employee surveys
- Customer surveys/insight studies
- Non-customer surveys
- Financial statements
- Marketing ROI analysis
- Marketing segmentation
- KPIs (key performance indicators)
- Customer advisory boards

EXTERNAL SOURCES

- Market intelligence
- Supplier feedback
- Government statistics
- Blogs/Trade press
- Trade associations
- Competitive websites
- Competitive web traffic
- Benchmarking

EXAMPLES OF KEY DATA INPUTS INCLUDE:

Financial Projections. Look for information that may not normally be presented in a financial statement. For example, it is useful to graph the key elements of an income statement over time. Most businesses have several important financial levers, including sales and marketing or research and development investment. By charting such variables over time one can see potential lift of such investments:

	2017F		2018		2019	
Revenue by Segment						
US	$27,000,000	99.26%	$30,000,000	93.75%	$34,500,000	93.24%
International	$200,000	0.74%	$1,000,000	3.13%	$1,250,000	3.38%
New Products	$0	0.00%	$1,000,000	3.13%	$1,250,000	3.38%
Total Revenue (by segment)	$27,200,000		$32,000,000		$37,000,000	
Y.O.Y. Revenue Growth			17.60%		15.60%	
Gross Margin ($)	$10,500,000		$13,000,000		$14,874,000	
Gross Margin (%)	38.60%		40.60%		40.20%	
Sales and Marketing Expenses	10.00%		10.00%		10.00%	
GA Expenses	15.00%		14.80%		14.00%	
EBITDA	$3,700,000		$5,056,000		$5,999,400	
% of Revenue	13.60%		15.80%		16.20%	

Download the Financial Projections Guide at:
www.optimizeinc.net/downloads

VALUE DRIVER:
FINANCIAL HEALTH

Value Driver Tip—Chart out five-year projections including key contributors to EBITDA, such as sales and marketing.

Employee Feedback. Too often, entrepreneurs maximize the value of strategic input from mid-managers or frontline employees. Typically, companies survey employees about their satisfaction, yet solicit little feedback about possible improvements to products and services.

Given the war for talent, finding ways of leveraging employee contributions is gaining importance. Additionally, frontline employees are closest to customers and often have the best insight into how a company can deliver more value.

Customer Insight Studies and Customer Advisory Boards. Our firm routinely completes such studies for clients that want to learn why customers—especially B2B customers—buy. There are three methods to gather such information: panels, primary research and secondary research.

Gathering customer feedback is a bit of a self-fulfilling prophecy, because asking for feedback increases loyalty. However, customer satisfaction has been marginalized, and to gain truly useful feedback requires either the "higher touch" offered by an independent firm calling customers or similar effort that yields actionable insights. The point of such an exercise should be to answer questions such as *Where do we go from here?* and *How will the client's business change in the future?*

Benchmarking. Gathering benchmarks provides feedback on various financial ratios. Companies principally want to know what their competitors spend on labor, sales and marketing. But the true value in benchmarking is understanding the point at which a company's overhead can be absorbed at a higher rate (providing high profit).

It is useful to benchmark with a company that matches your size. Although several services provide such information, often it is organized by U.S. government NAICS codes, which do not always reflect the nature of a specific business. For example, there may be a NAICS code for food production or for cookies and crackers, but not one for rice cakes.

External Data Points. Companies use a number of databases—like Gartner for technology—for external research, which tend to be expensive. Some excellent information on industry growth rates can be found for free on U.S. government websites.

CHAPTER REVIEW

▸ Companies often make decisions without data.

▸ Management teams can evaluate their momentum through market share, penetration or total addressable market.

▸ Market research, like strategic planning, is imperfect. Yet some information is better than no information.

▸ Primary research is research conducted for the first time.

▸ Secondary research is repurposed from existing sources.

▸ Companies should have ongoing awareness of their financial health, including five-year projections of key variables that contribute to EBITDA.

Tools Offered in this Chapter:

Financial Projections Guide
www.optimizeinc.net/downloads

Chapter 7
GOING ALL IN—THE INTEGRATED SALES AND MARKETING SYSTEM

"Asking the right question is 95 percent
of getting the right answer."
—Charlie Rose

THE RULES OF ENGAGEMENT for sales and marketing are undergoing rapid transformation. Globalization and hyper-competition have extended the reach of professional procurement. Industries including food distribution and aerospace are dominated by buying organizations whose sole purpose is to reduce prices, even at the cost of quality. Less mature industries that have not yet been subject to professional procurement are likely to be in for a rude awakening.

Relationship selling and traditional marketing approaches have given way to a new way of doing business. In many industries, customers will settle for "just-good-enough" in terms of product performance, quality or service.

This environment has promoted a new reality: Only the strongest will survive. Winning B2B vendors will:

- Have the best-in-class value proposition and provide end-to-end solutions
- Have the size and sophistication to fulfill requirements for systems integrations, supply chain and compliance
- Have fully integrated sales and marketing platforms that allow for mastery of targeting, messaging and consultative selling
- Embrace marketing as a critical component in the customer acquisition process. Social media has become the soundtrack for the next generation of buyers, and the most sophisticated sellers will find new ways to reach and convert them

As most of our clients have been small and mid-market, they are often constrained in their sales and marketing investment. One might run an ecommerce/call center operation with heavy online marketing and no outside salespeople. The next may be a B2B parts supplier with an outside sales presence that has no marketing function at all. Salespeople often do their own marketing, even though they have no expertise in marketing. Many companies seem to be more opportunistic than comprehensive, in terms of their sales and marketing capabilities.

Suppliers can no longer win on reputation alone; they must have the full complement of resources to win and keep customers.

> 💡 *A deficit in some entrepreneurial companies: There can be a lack of synergy between sales and marketing. If the company is sales heavy, it may have a sales VP who may or may not understand marketing. In some companies marketing and sales barely talk to one another. Step one is ensuring that marketing and sales have common goals and work collaboratively to ensure conversion and sales productivity.*

The confluence of data analytics, market research, CRM, marketing automation, social media and other tools creates

more opportunity than ever for marketers to design meaningful campaigns that deliver sales impact. As we explored earlier, hyper-competition begets hyper-segmentation and sales teams looking for an edge need to be supported by marketing efforts that target specific groups of customers.

As Jim Collins taught us, a useful value proposition can be created by offering products that we are passionate about, are within our core competency and are meaningful in the marketplace. One of the most common problems we see is poor targeting. Only after a company has designated specific target markets can sales and marketing identify specific potential customer groups and individual targets. Every company must have a model to assess the value of potential customers. We have illustrated such a model in a target value diagram:

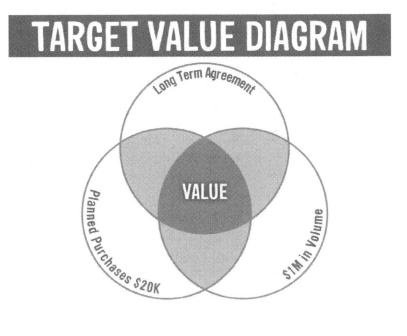

A target value diagram may represent the attributes of a company's best customers and prospects. Each prospect can then be put through a value fitness test exercise:

VALUE FITNESS TEST

				POTENTIAL VALUE	SCORE
Long Term Agreement	YES	NO		YES=20, NO=0	20
Professional Procurement	YES	NO		YES=0, NO=10	0
Engineering or Design Solutions	YES	NO		YES=10, NO=0	10
Stated Performance Criteria	YES	NO		YES=5, NO=0	5
Annual Review with Management	YES	NO		YES=5, NO=0	5
Annual Volume	$600-800K	$800-999K	>$1M	6-12	12
Order Size	>$10K	>$15K	>$20K	4-15	8
Number of Products	>10	>15	>20	5-10	10
Lead Time	7 DAYS	10 DAYS	21 DAYS	0-5	3
Terms	60	45	30	0-4	0
Likely to Pay within Terms	YES	NO		YES=5, NO=0	0
TOTAL					73

In this case, the prospect has a score of 73, meeting the company's minimum fitness score of 70.

Such criteria can be used to value existing clients as well. The discipline of matching prospects and customers based on suitability could be thought of as "managing inside-out."

Download the Value Diagram and Fitness Test templates at *www.optimizeinc.net/downloads*

> 💡 *In establishing their value proposition, companies can either align with the purchase triggers of their customers or focus on what they value most (inside-out).*

A model can be created that illustrates the attributes present in A clients (middle of the circle), B clients, etc.

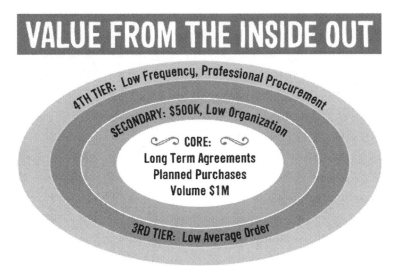

Such an evaluation can be made of entire vertical markets as well.

	Commercial	Defense	Consumer
LTA	Low	Hi	Low
Planned Purchases	Low	Hi	Mid
Volume	Hi	Mid	Hi

Arguably, selling inside-out protects margins because the provider can focus on attributes other than price. However, it requires a consultative skill set on the part of salespeople, and truly consultative salespeople are hard to come by.

The contemporary salesperson must be capable of navigating highly sophisticated buying environments, especially in B2B. One cannot overstate how difficult business development has become in a low growth environment. The bottom 75 percent of salespeople are reduced to buying business based on price. It's estimated that the best performing salespeople outsell average performers by 50–200 percent.

Several factors can contribute to flat revenue growth, many of which are the topics of this book: poor strategy, poor value proposition, lack of synergy in sales and marketing or poor execution. When revenue growth erodes, it is all too convenient to blame the salespeople.

Of course, professional procurement is designed to remove subjectivity and risk from the process. Buyers today are not interested in partnership; they want the best product, the best terms and the best price. They are experts at "framing."

Framing occurs when one party manages the nature of the relationship for the other. In professional procurement, it is the buyers' game, their field, their uniforms, their bat and their umpire. It is hard to win. Framing appears in every relationship—even in the absence of professional procurement.

If a salesperson attempts to visit the customer, she is often given twenty minutes to meet with a midlevel manager in a generic buying office. Visual cues—pictures of the buyer's family, or a college degree hanging in his or her office—have purposely been removed from the equation. Everything about the relationship is communicated as "me buyer," "you seller."

Organizations—and not just their salespeople—should be doing everything in their power to reframe. The contemporary salesperson, understanding this, challenges the buyer to the core.

One of our clients is a large aerospace manufacturer with a novel business strategy; they work with only twenty-five customers. They are not shy about telling customers and prospects this. With nearly 100 percent on-time delivery and quality, they pull the carpet out from under buyers who don't provide reasonable terms. New prospects are vetted and taken on as customers if they are a better fit than an existing customer. It is remarkable how customers respond to the "takeaway."

The company has managed its framing very well. It does not put its salespeople in a position where they are subservient to the customer. Salespeople can problem-solve, negotiate and communicate with buyers as peers.

As discussed in our previous example, the aerospace industry is first about quality and on-time delivery. This is the cost of admission vendors must master before going to the next step in a negotiation. The takeaway works because these companies have a fractured procurement base (many vendors) that struggles to meet their unyielding requirements. When a vendor is late, they are fired and replaced by another. The reason we have used aerospace examples in this section is because it is a mature industry, and other industries will adopt these principles as they move down the industry life cycle.

Senior sales management within an organization is responsible for ensuring that a company can frame its offer well and put its salespeople in a position to win. Sales management is also undergoing a sea change. Today, the contemporary sales manager must possess the following critical skills:

- Have a seat at the table for strategy, ensuring that the company's business model, products and services are highly relevant, i.e., enabling proper framing
- Enable salespeople to be highly effective in each customer relationship by providing the right tools, including training, and the marketing support needed to win in a hypercompetitive environment
- Manage the pipeline, understand the company's momentum, and keep abreast of opportunities with specific customers
- Act as if they are responsible for the company's sales results and hold salespeople accountable to performance outcomes

One of the biggest contributors to poor sales results is a misalignment between the business strategy and the sales team. In their book *The Challenger Sale*, authors Matthew Dixon and Brent Adamson point out the various selling styles employed by salespeople.[39] Although labels such as "hunter" and "farmer" are often used, they are overly simplistic in understanding styles that may best align with a strategy.

Dixon and Adamson categorized selling style into five buckets with "challenger" salespeople being the most consultative. When there was some complexity in the products or services they were selling, challengers comprised 20 percent of the total and represented 54 percent of the top-performing salespeople.

Highly sophisticated selling environments require salespeople who can behave like a teacher and coach, sharing information, often of a technical nature. They must "take control" of the sale. They are also master collaborators, consulting within their own companies to solve problems. These people are equally adept at convincing a customer they should buy as they are at convincing the ops guy that a three-day lead time is possible.

In less sophisticated environments—such as a call center—such an approach would be less effective than traditional relationship selling. Different elements of the selling process may require both sets of competencies.

As discussed in Chapter 4, best-in-class companies are constantly evolving their business model, and moving toward participating in more steps in the value chain. It is for this reason that consultative salespeople deliver more value to customers and their employer. They are not focused on transactions, but on ensuring that their product or service has been customized to meet customer needs. Thus, they must also be excellent consultants within their own companies, prodding customer service, operations, engineering, design and marketing to tweak the model to delight customers.

Earlier in my career I led business development for a food company in the grocery industry. Professional procurement had already bastardized the category, and for most vendors the industry had been reduced to a real estate war—that is, who was willing to pay the exorbitant slotting fees. Our company had a pretty dynamic value proposition with several critical components. But we really won with information. We had the best data, analytics and reporting. The salespeople for our competition didn't have a chance.

Salespeople must have the tools to win. For them to be consultative and command the highest prices and fees, they must have access to information: white papers, case studies and business intelligence. These tools are not a supplement to a successful sales team; they are an inherent element of the sales process.

One of the most pivotal skills the contemporary salesperson must have is the ability to navigate sensitive price conversations, and to reframe the conversation. If a company has the right business model, and the sales relationship is framed correctly, there should be room for a salesperson to discuss change orders, rushed shipments, price increases and other circumstances that promote higher margins.

When salespeople are unable to have difficult conversations about price increases and the like, it reflects more fundamental problems with the customer relationship, either because of poor framing or performance as a vendor. Finally, if service and quality are part of the brand promise, the supplier must execute flawlessly.

VALUE DRIVER:
SALES COMPETENCY AND
CUSTOMER RELATIONSHIPS

Value Driver Tip—Enable sales success through a fully integrated sales and marketing system. Both functions should report to the same manager, unless marketing is a core competency with an entire organization supporting it.

The world of marketing is also under siege. As companies focus on return on marketing investment (ROMI), they have moved away from conventional advertising and toward the use of less expensive, yet valuable digital assets. Some veteran marketers are having difficulty adapting to this new world.

Within the shift to digital there are powerful trends guiding investment:

- The adoption of marketing automation tools such as HubSpot, Marketo and Pardot. These tools allow companies to drive search engine optimization (SEO), tracking of visitors, thought leadership and conversion
- Both B2C and B2B companies are shifting huge chunks of marketing spend to digital and mobile solutions
- Greater specialization within the marketing function, reflecting the need to have expertise in social media, PR, graphic design, web, and creation of content

A study conducted by *Chief Executive Magazine* illustrates the actual spend by sector. The study confirms that investment in sales and marketing varies dramatically by industry.

Consider the behavior within three distinct industries:

% of Revenue	Sales	Marketing Staff	Marketing Spend
Manufacturing	8%	2%	2%
Construction	5%	1%	1%
Software	21%	6%	5%

The pattern, especially in B2B businesses, is that sales investment is about three to four times that of marketing spend. Generally speaking, we believe sales spend is over weighted, and marketing under weighted. Of course, the dynamics of each industry dictate what type of investment is warranted. When conversion ratios are high, for example, and marketers are successfully tracking online activity and creating leads, a case could be made for greater investment.

For example, in software, where so many companies are shifting toward SaaS (software as a service), the passive income generated by any new sale dramatically reduces acquisition cost. In other words, if a salesperson generates a $20,000 deal in the current year that reoccurs for five years, its true acquisition is only $4,000 per year. Thus software companies, which are highly scalable, are incentivized to invest more heavily in sales and marketing because of the long tail of their revenue.

Unfortunately, CRM has been a four-letter word for some, given the horror stories of integrations gone wrong. CRMs are viewed by many as costly, time consuming and administrative.

However, all the best sales managers I know cannot function without one. That's because a functional CRM provides a systematic tracking of all of a company's sales activity, and easy reporting of the results. CRM with strong integration provides other benefits, including easy access to segment-specific information and more. CRM systems have become so critical because such solutions are the apex of the sales and marketing revolution.

CRM's ability to integrate sales activity and marketing automation in a way that provides real-time analytics is the key to true integration.

You could think of sales and marketing as an ecosystem, with several important moving parts. If you pour pollution in the river upstream, it pollutes everything downstream.

CRM is meaningless without a sales team that leverages it. Social media won't work unless someone can provide the content. Content such as white papers are not useful if the marketer cannot capture client information online.

How much should be spent on marketing? In developing a sales and marketing budget, management teams should ask questions to clarify spending decisions:

- How does our sales and marketing strategy align with our business goals?
- How will marketing and sales work together to create synergy and economic value?
- What is an acceptable return on investment?

- How much should the marketing budget be?
- Where and how should the money be allocated?

Other considerations for marketing spend include:

OUTLINE COSTS.

List sales and marketing on multiple lines on the P&L so that true costs are not masked or distorted. It is important to track ROI of both sales and marketing over several years.

Set aside adequate spending for digital assets, including an annual refresh of your website with dynamic design. Ensure that you have content, including testimonials, white papers and case studies to support your position. Video is a particularly important component of the digital toolbox.

ASSESS THE PERFORMANCE OF YOUR EXISTING MARKETING AND SALES.

One useful tool for measuring the effectiveness of your marketing and sales is the Selling Expense Productivity Ratio (SEPR), which assesses revenue generated for every dollar spent on sales and marketing. Although it may be difficult to compare your SEPR vs. that of other companies, you can track increases each year to determine additional spending. When your SEPR increases, additional investment may be warranted.

Another way to view the ratio is through acquisition cost. Naturally, companies must measure their acquisition cost and find an appropriate equilibrium for their investment. The attributes of acquisition cost may vary, and a simple way to measure is by dividing the selling expense by the number of new customers, assuming salespeople do not service existing businesses. (In that case, calculate the estimated time they spend selling to new customers.) For example:

Acquisition Cost = Selling Costs $3,000,000 \ New Customers 150 = $20,000 (per customer)

SEPR (Margin) = Selling Costs $3,000,000 \ Lifetime Value of New Margin Dollars $7,000,000 = 43 percent

This is one reason we're seeing more spend on Search Engine Optimization (SEO) and the like. The Return on Marketing Investment (ROMI) is much higher with SEO than with traditional marketing methods. Of course, in some businesses, SEO has little or no impact if clients found online deliver little value.

Allocate budget for sales and service.

Management teams should recognize that there is a base budget required to protect existing volume, and a different level of spending required to generate incremental volume (new business). It is rare that account managers will spend adequate time in business development. A company's budget, organization and incentive plans should address both client service and client acquisition.

Develop a Sales Scorecard.

Develop a sales scorecard that measures new customer sales, SEPR or acquisition costs. (See more on this below.) Ensure that both your sales and marketing teams understand investments and are accountable for results.

CHAPTER REVIEW

- In some entrepreneurial companies there is a lack of synergy between sales and marketing. Make sure marketing and sales have common goals, and work collaboratively to ensure conversion and sales productivity.

- In establishing their value proposition, companies can either align with the purchase triggers of the customer or focus on what they value most (inside-out).

- Customer Relationship Management's (CRM) ability to integrate sales activity and marketing automation, in a way that provides real-time analytics, is the next frontier in sales and marketing.

- Think of sales and marketing as an ecosystem, with several important moving parts. If you pour pollution in the river upstream, it pollutes everything downstream.

- Framing occurs when one party manages the nature of the relationship for the other. In professional procurement, it is the buyer's game, their field, their uniforms, their bat and their umpire. It's hard to win.

- Growth companies enable sales success through fully integrated sales and marketing systems.

- CRM is meaningless without a sales team that leverages it. Social media won't work unless someone can provide the content. White papers may not provide a marketer with much information unless the papers' information is captured online.

Tools Offered in this Chapter:

The Value Diagram and Fitness Test templates
www.optimizeinc.net/downloads

Chapter 8
THE PEOPLE

"In a few hundred years, when the history of our time
will be written from a long-term perspective, it is likely
that the most important event historians will see is
not technology, not the Internet, not e-commerce. It is
an unprecedented change in the human condition.
For the first time—literally—substantial and rapidly
growing numbers of people have choices. For the
first time, they will have to manage themselves.
And society is totally unprepared for it."
—Peter Drucker

N MY SPEAKING ENGAGEMENTS around North America,
I talk to hundreds of executives every year who gripe about
their inability to attract and retain talent. Even before the
recent uptick toward full employment, employers were having
difficulty finding skilled labor, or even reliable hourly labor.

There are massive shortages for roles ranging from welders to data scientists.

> 💡 *Developing human capital is the most significant barrier to scale in many organizations.*

Things are going to get a lot worse. According to Pew Research (and published in the *Wall Street Journal*), a staggering 45 million baby boomers are within five years of the traditional retirement age. Workers with fewer than twelve years of experience comprise more than a third of the workforce. It is a simple math problem—there are not enough experienced workers to fill the funnel.

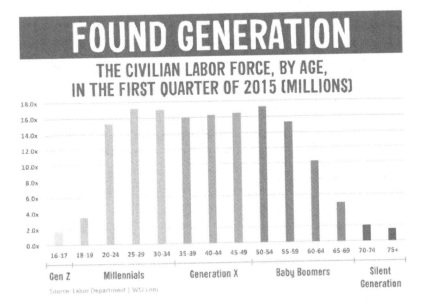

FOUND GENERATION

THE CIVILIAN LABOR FORCE, BY AGE, IN THE FIRST QUARTER OF 2015 (MILLIONS)

Source: Labor Department | WSJ.com

There are several other employment trends that are alarming:

- The labor participation rate in the United States dropped to 63 percent in 2016.[40]
- Although older boomers held an average of 11.7 jobs between the ages of eighteen and forty-eight, those born in the 1980s held 7.2 jobs from age eighteen through twenty-eight.[41]
- The average tenure in the United States is 4.2 years, down from 4.6, declining ten percent in just two years.
- Seventy-nine percent of millennials have student loans that "have a moderate or significant impact on their ability to meet their other financial goals".[42]
- According to Gallup, millennials are by far the least engaged employees (29 percent).
- According to Deloitte, 89 percent of executives cite "developing leaders" as a high priority, but only 13 percent say they are excellent at creating them.

So, there are fewer people looking for work, they have less tenure and loyalty and are under immense financial pressure. What could go wrong? Meanwhile, employment costs have skyrocketed as a result of spiraling health care costs and higher minimum wages in urban centers, especially in the West.

These are trends that are most troubling when you consider the age group from which employers typically find their management workers. Those employees with five to eight years of experience, and the life skills necessary to lead, tend to be in their thirties. These employees will be in high demand under this set of demographic realities.

These demographic conditions will only magnify the existing labor shortage. Clearly, those companies who have the best talent are going to have a significant strategic advantage over those who do not. Every element in a company's strategy, including product development, marketing and technology, is driven by people.

Further, I would suggest we are trying to solve problems using a dated playbook. It is no different than the United States using conventional warfare tactics against counterinsurgencies around the world. As in those wars, this war for talent will require boots on the ground and the right campaign to win over hearts and minds.

Most companies employ the same tired script for HR:

- Hire one HR generalist for every 80–130 people
- Then, hire a VP
- Have those people cover everything—from payroll, to wage-and-hour compliance, to benefits
- Implement a Human Resources Information System (HRIS)
- Offer basic training and management classes

- Build an employer web page, with a list of openings
- Administer performance management

It's not hard to understand why this script is falling woefully short. Today's contemporary workers are looking for much more than a paycheck, or even skills acquisition. They want to connect to something bigger than them—to be aligned with a purpose. Command and control is a thing of the past. Our business culture is moving toward tribes and networks and away from hierarchical management systems.

HR as a function is also undergoing a seismic shift. Specialized skills are required to succeed in this war. For example, today's environment requires online recruiters with social media savvy. One reason companies don't have the right people in the right seats on the bus is that their HR people are not in the right seats. If there is a war for talent, we need all hands on deck.

VALUE DRIVER:
RIGHT PEOPLE IN THE RIGHT SEATS

Value Driver Tip—Growth companies must position themselves as employers of choice. That includes a maniacal focus on culture, and the ability to communicate values and vision to employees and applicants.
Over and above winning an award or certification, growth companies need to be best-in-class.

Why is it so many employees seem apathetic toward their employers? A contributor to this problem is that the prototypical employment model is completely broken.

It starts with bad hiring. Given the dearth of skilled workers, some companies are somewhat desperate. Lacking a true employer brand, they reach for B and C players. B and C players hire other B and C players, and the domino effect takes over and spirals out of control.

The traditional hiring model is particularly troubling. In most companies, a hiring manager posts an open role through HR. HR conducts an external search, typically through job boards. Job boards are the worst source for candidates (especially at a time of full employment), because only the dregs of the workforce are applying there.

After finding a short list, HR conducts phone interviews, and passes on final candidates to a hiring manager. Then perhaps HR and the hiring manager conduct one-hour face-to-face interviews. We then judge a person's abilities and fit based on what we see and hear in a one-hour interaction. We all know that behavior is more important than skill, but the clear focus in these interactions is to assess capabilities, and technical knowledge.

Many will say they interview for "fit," but my experience is that fewer than 20 percent of interview questions focus on playing well with others. We hire for fit but interview for skills.

Over the last decade we have been advocating that our clients utilize the Topgrading model, originally offered by Brad and Geoff Smart through their breakthrough research and book—*Topgrading (How to Hire, Coach and Keep A Players)*.

The Topgrading methodology favors a team hiring approach:

- Companies should be looking for people 24/7/365—whether they need them or not
- All managers should be sourcing candidates on a regular basis
- When necessary, recruiters with deep databases should be used to mine candidates
- When interviews are conducted, many managers should be involved in the process. Group hiring promotes specialization. Each manager can probe deeper on a topic such as communication or desktop skills and vet the candidate's true capabilities
- Candidates should be formally scored, with observations shared in a face-to-face meeting of the hiring team
- Skills and personality testing should be completed when appropriate
- Significant, peer-to-peer references should be completed, such as a Director of Ops calling candidates' past Director of Ops

To download our Staffing Plan Guide, go to: *www.optimizeinc.net/downloads*

Managers will justify their lack of attention to such details by saying they don't have time. Yet employee turnover is incredibly costly, not only in terms of hard costs but in terms of quality, customer satisfaction and the like. There is simply no good business case for taking hiring lightly.

Managers also tend to hire for skill sets that do not represent the requirements of the contemporary workforce. What is emerging is the reality that the single most important skill set today is the ability to adapt. Adaptability is difficult to ascertain in a job interview.

After hiring employees, we often do not provide them with a roadmap for success. In advance of strategic planning, we conduct organizational surveys of managers. Management teams regularly report inadequate onboarding of new employees. It is estimated that 52 percent of turnover happens within the first year of employment.[43]

Published turnover rates are drastically understated, at least in part because of the many different methods companies use to calculate turnover. It's estimated that fewer than ten percent of companies calculate their turnover costs (including indirect costs). According to the Bureau of Labor Statistics, the monthly separations rate tends to run at about 3.4 percent per month or 40 percent per year.

In many companies, onboarding is entirely unstructured. After the initial HR orientation (where an employee's first experience with an employer is to fill out forms with HR), we feed them to the wolves. Each department employs a different onboarding protocol. This is not only confusing, but unproductive.

Each new employee should have a clear path for success in his or her new role. Many of our clients use a 90-Day Plan. For white collar jobs, onboarding should start with cultural immersion and an education about the company's strategic plan and management goals. This is best done by the CEO—sometimes via video or webinar. Then, managers should have several weeks of training, including cross-training with other departments.

For high-turnover entry level jobs, there may be less time in training, but there should be significant structure. For example, every skill needed in a technical position should be reviewed. Both the new employee and trainer—this can be a group of colleagues—should sign off when each skill has been demonstrated and mastered.

The good news is that these methods are so widespread that employers of choice can truly create competitive advantage by ensuring that prospects and new employees have a great experience. A provocative metric is new hire satisfaction, an excellent way to measure your management team's hiring performance.

In particular, executives point to their issues in hiring and retaining younger workers—that is to say, millennials. We cannot ignore the importance of mastering the hiring and onboarding of younger workers, for two reasons. First, they are probably smarter than us. They grew up during a time when schools were more competitive in subjects like math and science, and their ability to adapt and use technology is unmatched by my generation. Second, the demographic shifts underway afford us no choice.

In the book *The Alliance: Managing Talent in the Networked Age*, Ben Casnocha, Reid Hoffman and Chris Yeh offer fresh insight on how to recruit and retain millennials. They cite millennials having the perception that employment is like a "tour of duty," and recommend that employers embrace this concept and openly discuss the employment goals of people who could potentially leave.

I have found that employers are so afraid that young workers may leave that they stop investing in skills acquisition for them. Ironically, this is one of the most important benefits desired by these workers.

Imagine a conversation with a millennial that looks something like this. Question: "What would you like your next job to be?" Based on the answer, ask for a commitment. "If I help you acquire the skills you need over the next three to four years, and promise to assist you in your next job search, can I have your full attention during that time? At the end of your tour we can both reevaluate, and you decide if you would like to re-up for another tour."

This way of thinking is alien to most employers but offers the greatest possibility of achieving engagement with a young worker who needs to feel their employer truly has their best interest at heart.

More broadly, employers are afraid to have career discussions with their employees, because they believe they cannot fulfill their employees' desire to advance. This is especially true in flat, family-run organizations where there are few advancement opportunities. But embracing the "tour of duty" concept enables a different type of mentality. Such conversations should be about skills acquisitions the employee can use to advance his or her career.

Perhaps the most important ingredient missing in most companies is a lack of connectivity to employees. Employees do not feel that they are part of something larger than they are. This is why the annual Gallup Poll consistently reveals shockingly low engagement numbers with employees.

I have witnessed two attributes in management teams that value culture. First, they really do live the behaviors that are expected, and demand that their teams do so as well.

Second, they reinforce the importance of mission, values and behaviors constantly. Visual management tools can be used to drive the message home:

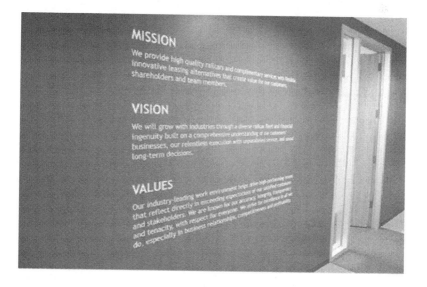

Such tools demonstrate a company's focus and commitment to these statements and make them a tangible part of a working environment.

Companies should go one step further and convert values into behaviors. For example, a common value is integrity. But integrity may mean different things to different people. A behavior that highlights integrity would be to always share information with colleagues and clients—even when it could be hurtful.

Mission>Values>Behaviors

Values and behaviors should be used as a barometer. When an employee is not behaving in alignment with company values, he or she must be called out (privately, of course).

Succession planning and building career paths are not only important for employee retention but also as best practices for building a successful and sustainable business. Shockingly, many family businesses we have worked with, with executives in their fifties or sixties, do not discuss succession out of fear of alienating their parents or siblings. Families will put assets that can be worth hundreds of millions of dollars at risk out of their fear of conflict.

In our practice we advocate that every manager have an identified successor. Generally, we promote an open dialogue about succession, but there are certainly instances when it makes more sense to keep such discussions private.

However, succession discussions create the impetus for a company's most promising employees to gain clarity about how and where they can improve skill sets (whether they are technical or soft skills). We are also at a crossroads as employers in terms of work-life balance. Consider the following: The average amount of time that fathers talk to their children is seven minutes a day.[44] Thirty percent of working age Americans are obese.[45] Seventy million have a sleep disorder.[46]

Work-life balance is not some cool, trendy employment fad; it is a way of life. Those employers who truly understand the need to promote the wellness and happiness of their employees and reinforce that through strong employment branding will have a strategic advantage over those who don't.

On-demand labor, made popular by Uber, is here to stay as a viable employment practice. Today's collaboration tools (such as Slack and Wrike) provide new utility and new methods of working that promote greater flexibility and efficiency.

A critical component of a strategic plan is a staffing plan. At a minimum, the plan needs to formalize and quantify staffing levels by department, role and year. To create such a plan requires a meaningful evaluation of staff and future needs.

Another broken HR system is performance management. When I first launched my consulting firm, I thought I needed to have a product to sell. I created an integrated online platform for performance management and learning. We sold the product to several large companies, including a Fortune 1000 industry leader who had never seen its features gathered into one solution before.

Unfortunately, we were about a decade too early to market. I had to convince people that they should have an automated platform for measuring performance and assigning relevant learning. I grew impatient, sold off the code and moved on.

There has been a lot of controversy surrounding performance management of late. Managers are growing tired spending hours writing detailed reviews. Netflix and Deloitte have publicly cited their movement away from formalized performance reviews and toward informal performance loops.

Part of the revolution in performance management goes right back to the dynamic shift in demographics, and the fact that millennials clearly want regular feedback. Companies should consider replacing the stodgy annual performance review with a system that formalizes feedback but ensures its frequency.

Tying the review cycle to compensation is particularly troublesome. When employees associate being reviewed with garnering a raise, a dangerous entitlement is created that clouds the conversation around improvement.

Further, there is poor linkage in many reviews between an employee's performance and his or her future learning opportunities. Every employee should have a clear learning plan.

The training industry is also undergoing significant transformation. In the 2000s companies implemented costly and ineffective learning management systems, many under the premise that e-learning would offer more choice at a lower cost of ownership. It didn't work. E-learning has proven ineffective in teaching many skills (especially soft skills).

When left to their own devices, employees will not train. The only way to ensure the execution of learning plans is to structure their deployment and make them a requirement.

We recommend adopting a balanced approach to performance management and learning:

- Adopt a more streamlined formal performance review form. Complete it annually.

- Create a feedback loop with frequent communication to employees.
- Establish a learning plan for every employee.
- Conduct annual discussions about career path and succession.

It is time to move to a new playbook. To summarize:

Lead with purpose. There are two types of management teams—those that care about things like mission, values and vision statements and those who go through the motions. Take your words seriously and ensure your employees understand how their contributions align with a purpose bigger than themselves. Utilize employee engagement as a lever for differentiation with prospective employees.

Invest in strong employer branding. It is not good enough to be an employer of choice. Great employers tell their stories online through employee testimonials and the like. Videos are a powerful medium for illustrating your culture.

Reinforce your culture every day. Talking about culture is not enough. Management needs to ingrain celebration of culture into all management decisions. Remind employees again and again about the principles that are important to you.

Get HR out of the command center and onto the front line. If you are serious about being a great employer, invest in a world-class HR leader who will spend more time on culture and less on compliance. Any HR generalist can do that.

Over-communicate. Internal communications should be treated like external communication. Commonly, marketers must repeat the same message seven to ten times to be heard by a prospect or customer. Employers must repeat messaging over and over for cultural norms and behaviors to be ingrained in staff.

Provide the best environment. Although alternative work environments have spread like wildfire, there are still old-school managers who believe they must physically supervise their staff. If you don't provide the most inviting workspace and virtual environment, employees will gravitate elsewhere.

Embrace a continuous feedback loop. Conventional performance reviews are being replaced by more frequent feedback systems. Employees still want to see their employers take their evaluations seriously. And employees want consistent reinforcement. Utilize frequent one-on-one meetings to engage with them and keep them in the fold.

Get serious about building career paths and succession. Take the time to sit down with every employee to discuss their future.

Finally, there is another reason to be a great employer. Customers want to do business with employers of choice because they are perceived as better companies.

EIGHT STEPS FOR SUCCESSION

There are 27 million closely held businesses in the U.S., and it is estimated that there are roughly 5 million baby boomer business owners. Many of them will face a dilemma in years ahead—sell the business or pass it on to their heirs.

Only about a third of U.S. businesses make it to a second generation. Only 12 percent pass on to a third generation.[47] What is surprising about these numbers is that there is no shortage of family members working in these businesses. There is, however, a significant fear about having discussions about succession.

It appears that people do not like to talk about the death or incapacity of their aging parents and relatives. We don't like talking about it personally, much less within our businesses when there are economic ramifications. These problems seem to magnify when there are several siblings in a business fighting to maintain some pecking order.

Yet what these entrepreneurs fail to recognize is that failure to provide clarity about a succession plan creates stress for the business, their own children and their employees. Although such conversations may be unpleasant, and can even create strife within a family, the alternative can be much worse. Siblings compete for power and influence, putting employees in the impossible position of interpreting who they go to for what. We once worked with a husband and wife and their two children. It could take the four-headed monster months to make a decision, even on the most mundane things. The unwillingness of the parents to plan for succession created unnecessary dysfunction.

It doesn't have to be that way. One creates a will or trust not for oneself but to ease the pain of those who will have to manage their financial affairs someday. Creating a succession plan as well as the precursory financial and estate planning instruments is not that difficult. Family law offices and financial planners are adept at creating the necessary documentation.

Here are some steps to consider in creating a succession plan (for private companies and family held businesses):

STEP 1. SET SPECIFIC LONG-TERM GOALS FOR OWNERSHIP.

This is often achieved through some form of long-term planning process.

STEP 2. ESTABLISH A SET OF MANAGERIAL COMPETENCIES.

Focus on those things that are important in your operating environment, such as operational excellence, innovation or financial acumen.

STEP 3. EVALUATE THE MANAGEMENT TEAM.

Have the management team assess the skills of each manager or hire an outside firm to study his or her emotional intelligence and skill level. Create a grid and grade based on the resultant managerial competencies.

STEP 4. DEBRIEF THE ASSESSMENT.

Review the findings of the skills assessment and offer each manager specific development opportunities that will inform them on how they can progress during the course of their career.

STEP 5. SEEK OUT HIGH-QUALITY LEGAL AND TAX ADVICE.

Consider all legal and tax implications regarding the transfer of ownership or control. Remember that with outside advisors, you get what you pay for. Most business owners need a high-level CPA, transactional/estate attorney and wealth manager, all of whom work together as a brain trust.

STEP 6. CREATE A ROBUST PERFORMANCE MANAGEMENT SYSTEM.

Train your managers (especially senior managers) on how to hold people accountable to specific performance outcomes.

STEP 7. IDENTIFY THE SUCCESSORS.

Have frank (and confidential) conversations with your top people about their career path. Consider hiring a coach (or have them join an executive group like Vistage) to help them develop their skills. Ensure developing new leaders is a core competency in your company. Harness technology that will ensure critical success factors for contemporary executives.

STEP 8. HANDCUFF YOUR BEST PEOPLE.

Ensure that you have provided incentives for future senior managers to stick around.

To download our Succession Plan Form, go to: *www.optimizeinc.net/downloads*

As they say, a journey starts with a single step. Don't be afraid to have meaningful conversations about your succession plan. Then go find the professionals who can help you put your plan into action.

CHAPTER REVIEW

- ▶ Demographic trends will only magnify the U.S. labor shortage. Those companies that have the best talent are going to have a significant strategic advantage over those that don't. Every element in a company's strategy including product development, marketing, technology, and so forth, is driven by people.

- ▶ We are working from a dated playbook. Every company needs to have a campaign to win over employee hearts and minds.

- ▶ Growth companies must be employers of choice, with a maniacal focus on culture, great hiring and professional development.

- ▶ Be serious about building employee career paths and succession.

Tools Offered in this Chapter:

To download the Staffing Plan form, go to *www.optimizeinc.net/downloads*

To download the Succession Plan form, go to *www.optimizeinc.net/downloads*

Part II

HOW TO CREATE A STRATEGIC PLAN

Chapter 9
THE STRATEGY
ROADMAP

"Things which matter most must never be
at the mercy of things which matter least."
—Johann Wolfgang von Goethe

IN THIS CHAPTER WE PROVIDE a how-to guide for creating
a meaningful, thorough strategic plan. As mentioned in the
Foreword, some expected outcomes of strategic planning
should be to:

- Clarify a company's strategic objectives
- Establish a clear path for growth
- Unify the management team
- Set clear goals for management, to which they can
  be held accountable

- Prioritize investments such as the implementation of an ERP or opening a new factory that could drain capital and resources
- Create a foundation for key performance indicators
- Promote fact-based decision making based on data
- Promote transparency
- Provide a foundation for departmental and individual goal setting and incentive plans

Less than a third of U.S. companies formalize their strategic planning process. Even fewer use a professional facilitator. Few companies truly make the investment to be best-in-class when it comes to planning.

In my travels I hear two common rationalizations about why companies should not invest in formal strategic planning:

- We don't have time
- The minute we write the plan, it will be irrelevant

Stephen Covey, author of *The Seven Habits of Highly Effective People* (maybe the most important business book of all time), used to share a model about time. He illustrated the time and energy expended within a company as a circle. We spend part of our time planning and part of our time reacting. He claimed that the greater the portion of time spent planning, the smaller the pie.

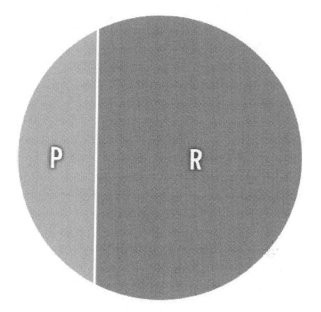

This is because when we are in a reactionary state, we are wasting time. When reacting, we make mistakes like shipping the wrong product, experiencing defects and generally doing the wrong thing for our customers. It is when we are thoughtful and patient that we do our best work, yielding our best products and work quality.

Let's apply this theory to a typical mid-market company. Say the company has six senior managers and 100 employees. Further, imagine this company were to spend 200 hours per year (33 hours per manager) in thoughtful deliberation about what markets to enter, what products or services to sell and what resources (people, processes and technology) are required to support growth.

If one were to rationalize that there is not enough time for planning, I would pose the following challenge. If the company's 100 employees worked an average of 2,000 hours per year, that would equal a total labor spend of 200,000 hours.

If the management team spent 200 hours in strategic planning, that would be .001 percent of the company's labor spend. Is it not worth .001 percent of a company's time to decide how to spend 200,000 labor hours? If you accept Covey's premise that planning makes the circle smaller, having no time for planning is an entirely illogical argument. In fact, I would say it's an excuse.

The second rationalization I hear is that the world is a volatile place. Managers say they cannot predict what is going to happen next month, much less next year. In my mind, that is a reason to plan more often. In fact, the behavior of companies is to have more frequent planning sessions, so they can react to the changing market conditions.

Strategic planning should be a cycle and not an activity.

Companies that have never completed a strategic plan should get one under their belt before trying to perfect a cycle, regardless of the time of year. Generally speaking, companies should attempt to complete a plan in advance of their budgetary cycle.

> A well-organized strategic planning cycle has a rhythm and cadence. The management team sets a long-term vision and a set of intermediate objectives and actions for the following year. They execute the plan. The following year they repeat the process, moving long-term goals and objectives forward by a year.

SETTING THE TONE

Strategic conversations can be severely compromised in a management team that lacks trust. There are behaviors that constrain a team's effectiveness in formulating strategy.

In such instances, team members:

- Include only a select few in making decisions
- Report on decisions instead of including a broad group in the decision-making process
- Engage in "false agreement," claiming they agree, when some don't truly buy in
- Create alliances with other managers to usurp authority
- Talk about other managers behind their backs
- Water down feedback with employees and supervisors
- Attack data as inaccurate
- State un-researched positions as facts
- Evade accountability
- Are unwilling to admit weakness
- Promote military style, top-to-bottom hierarchy
- Fail to create cascading goals and alignment

- Avoid vigorous debate on things they perceive as injurious to them
- Hire low-quality talent to preserve their own positions

For strategy to work well, managers need to overcome these tendencies and create a circle of trust. Some management teams may take part in team building to ensure that they overcome such problems. Strategic planning supports better team building as managers buy in to common goals.

At the onset of every strategy meeting, certain ground rules should be set. Managers must be willing to:

- Be entirely present (not on their laptops or phones)
- Commit to not enter into "false agreement"
- Engage in candid, unfettered, frank dialogue

Who Should Participate in Strategic Planning?

We recommend two criteria for deciding who should participate in strategy discussions:

- Who can be trusted with confidential strategic information?
- Who can think at a strategic level without getting mired in details?

Many of our clients err on the side of inclusion. Although we celebrate their desire to include managers in a process that could affect their work, there is also an optimal number of participants for such a meeting. Group dynamics are such that the ideal working group is eight to twelve people. There is a significant tradeoff when a meeting has more than twenty participants. Some people will not participate. There must be fewer topics discussed in large meetings, because there are more people with more to say.

There are other methods that enable employees to be inclusive and invite a broader range of opinions. We often conduct organizational surveys to ensure that managers and other stakeholders have the opportunity to contribute.

ELEMENTS OF STRATEGIC PLANNING: THE STRATEGY ROADMAP

So, what are the critical components of a strategic plan? The Strategy Roadmap is a tool that captures the essential elements of a strategic plan.

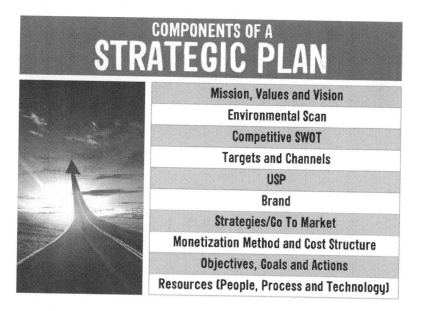

COMPONENTS OF A
STRATEGIC PLAN

| Mission, Values and Vision |
| Environmental Scan |
| Competitive SWOT |
| Targets and Channels |
| USP |
| Brand |
| Strategies/Go To Market |
| Monetization Method and Cost Structure |
| Objectives, Goals and Actions |
| Resources (People, Process and Technology) |

Download the Strategy Roadmap at
www.optimizeinc.net/downloads

Note: In some instances, the lines between these attributes
could be blurred. For example, a technology or group of technologies could be the source of a unique selling proposition.
For purposes of this exercise, we use the word technology to
describe the tactile usage of computers and systems to execute
a company's daily work.

**Below is a guide on how to think through each element,
so you can create a vision map and/or strategic plan.**

HOW TO CREATE MISSION, VALUES AND VISION STATEMENTS

Creating mission, values and vision statements are perhaps
the most fulfilling and difficult work that a management team
can undertake in the strategic planning process. As it relates
to creating these statements, there are two distinct camps:
those who care about them, and those who don't. I've seen
many management teams debate what these terms mean and
how they should be constructed.

Every management team should decide for itself which
statements apply and how they should be used. My observation has been that words do matter.

I once facilitated a strategic planning session for one of
the world's prominent speaker manufacturers. At one point
during the meeting the CEO practically pounded his fist on
the table and said, "We need to make products of uncompromised quality." The word "uncompromised" dictated much of

the business strategy: which products to make (and which to outsource), in what markets they should be sold, and at what price points. It informed what type of people they would hire, and what the marketing message would be. One single word was critical to the organization's future success.

Words can be important in terms of decision making, and can serve as a rallying cry for employees.

VALUE DRIVER:
UTILIZE MISSION, VALUES AND VISION STATEMENTS AS THE FOUNDATION OF LEADERSHIP AND CULTURE.

Value Driver Tip—Create a calendar of events that include monthly departmental or "all hands" meetings. These should feature spotlights, which demonstrate how employees have exemplified your values.

Given the rigorous debate on what mission, values and vision statements should mean, here is my take on the classical definitions:

The **mission statement** *articulates a company's purpose.* Mission transcends any product, service or short-term objective. It answers the question: Why are we here? Mission statements should be short (a sentence or two) and be the inspiration for the corporation and its employees. It is generally both inward and outward facing.

Values statements *are part of a core ideology that requires no justification from the outside world.* These are principles that embody the culture, and are essential in building a team.

The vision statement should state an alpha goal for the organization and a clear description of how it will get there. Mission statements are inspirational; vision statements are aspirational. They may include a destination or goal the company aspires to in the future. Vision statements can be outward-facing, but are often for internal consumption only.

TO REVIEW:

Mission states the company's purpose.

The **value statement** describes how people are to behave.

The **vision statement** articulates who we would like to become, or where we want to go.

> *Perhaps counterintuitive to people who don't value them, the adoption of mission, values and vision statements can drive economic value.*

If articulation of a vision is more likely to inspire a company to produce inventive products, it undoubtedly would have a financial impact.

If a clear articulation of values reduces the risk of employee attrition or safety events in the workplace, these same values could protect a company from financial risks. Given the war for talent, companies with strong retention execute better, interact with clients better and take part in a range of activities that improve their competitive advantage.

Below are methods for forming mission, values and vision statements.

HOW TO CRAFT THE MISSION STATEMENT.

Writing a mission statement can be a daunting task. Although there are no best practices or rules that prescribe what a mission statement must look like, it is typically consumed by both internal and external stakeholders, and should inspire a broad purpose. To create a meaningful mission statement, work with a small group, say six to eight people who understand the organization and its customers or stakeholders. If you have a large group in the strategic planning team, it may be better to create a draft in advance of your strategic planning meeting.

- Using a white board, capture the themes that best describe the company's core purpose.
- Discuss meaningful terms or themes that will inspire others.
- The mission statement must answer the question, Why? It may include the nature of the markets the company serves, as well as its general service or product categories. However, such details can dilute the statement and may be better in a vision statement. Some management teams will prefer to keep the statement vague in case the core of the business changes over time.
- Eliminate the least important themes.
- Try to develop a catchy description of the remaining themes.
- Keep the mission as short as possible (a sentence is often enough).
- Use simple language; there is no need to pontificate.

Examples of Mission Statements

Mission statements seek to inspire:

> Nike: *"To bring inspiration and innovation to every athlete in the world."*

Some mission statements explain what a company does in functional terms:

> Apple: *"Apple designs Macs, the best personal computers in the world, along with OS X, iLife, iWork and professional software. Apple leads the digital music revolution with its iPods and iTunes online store. Apple has reinvented the mobile phone with its revolutionary iPhone and App store, and is defining the future of mobile media and computing devices with iPad."*

> Our client, Justice Stores: *"To enhance a tween girl's self-esteem by providing her the hottest fashion and lifestyle products, in a unique, fun, interactive environment—all at a great value for mom."*

> Note: Some companies don't believe in mission statements at all and may instead create a very brief mantra that is 3-4 words.

HOW TO CRAFT A VALUES STATEMENT.

First, have your team create a list of words that describe how people should behave. This list usually uses words like integrity and honesty. Then, consolidate the list (for example, honesty could be viewed as a subset of integrity).

One of our favorite values sets is from our client, the Deschutes Brewery:

1. Honor our customers.
2. Deliver quality.
3. Work as a team.
4. Do our best and next time do it better.
5. Build a healthier society.
6. Celebrate the culture of beer.
7. Own it.

Many teams then choose to assign a statement to what each value means:

Integrity: We do what we say we will do at the time we say we will do it.

For our clients that place a premium on culture, values are not just words on a wall; they are a belief system. Key decisions are made using values as a barometer.

Some companies convert their values into "behaviors":

Integrity: We take responsibility for our mistakes, including informing clients of defects or late orders that may affect them.

There should be a limit to the number of values (generally no more than six or seven), so that every employee can live them and recite them on demand.

HOW TO CRAFT VISION STATEMENTS.

In terms of structure, vision statements are subject to the greatest debate. Vision statements should be forward-looking phrases that pinpoint a destination. They may or may not include specifics about products, markets, and so forth.

Our client, St. Barnabas Senior Services' vision statement:

"Every older adult ages in place and thrives in the community."

Often, the vision will be stated in a paragraph. It could be stated as:

"By 2025 ACME Widget Company will be the largest widget producer in North America, and named the top place to work in Milwaukee."

An important distinction between a mission statement and a vision statement is that the mission statement should rarely change based on the environment or business conditions, whereas the vision statement may be modified in the future.

EXTERNAL FACTORS

External factors, environmental factors and environmental scan are often used as interchangeable terms and reference trends external to a business and its industry. We recommend conducting a STEEP analysis, which is more rigorous than listing external threats and opportunities. By conducting a STEEP analysis, the strategists consider trends within the following five dimensions: Social, Technological, Economic, Ecological and Political. As discussed in Chapter 5, these are also the considerations for a scenario plan.

We strongly recommend that organizations consider external trends that may impact demand before completing a market analysis.

MARKET ANALYSIS

The market analysis considers conditions within an industry. There are many models for considering industry structure. Market analysis was born out of Michael Porter's "Five Forces" model.[48]

A brief review of Porter's model:

Threat of new entrants

The most profitable markets will attract new competitors. As new competitors enter a market, price pressure and margin erosion change the face of the industry.

Example of Mitigating Strategy:

Companies try to create barriers of entry such as patents or technologies.

Threat of substitutes

Today, substitute products are offered in the form of disruptive technologies, like Uber as a substitute for taxis.

Example of Mitigating Strategy:

Companies will attempt to create higher switching costs, such as multi-year agreements or exclusives.

Bargaining power of customers

Perhaps the most tenuous of market forces is the ability of customers to dictate price to vendors, because switching costs are low or they have access to many alternatives. The move toward cooperative buying and auctions magnifies bargaining power of customers.

Example of Mitigating Strategy:

Developing loyalty programs and total cost of ownership case studies.

Bargaining power of suppliers

Suppliers have greater pricing power when they provide specialized raw materials or skills.

Example of Mitigating Strategy:

Vertical integration of the value chain.

Industry rivalry

The culmination of these factors is industry rivalry, which reveals the competitiveness of the industry.

A market analysis combines these forces into a narrative about how the company fits into the market. In writing a market analysis, the strategist could consider questions such as:

- What are the industry needs?
- How are these forces shaping customer behavior?
- How fast is the industry growing?

- What types of companies are entering the market?
- What technologies are being adopted?
- What benchmarks (such as marketing spending) exist?

COMPETITIVE SWOT

Companies routinely complete an analysis of their strengths, weaknesses, opportunities and threats. Often, these are generic statements void of any true statistical basis. A meaningful SWOT analysis should reference actual trends supported by data.

It is important to note that depending on the industry, there could be crossover between environmental scan, market forces, STEEP and SWOT.

The accepted protocol for SWOT is:

- Strengths and weaknesses are internally focused
- Opportunities and threats are externally focused

An evaluation of internal strengths and weaknesses can be completed through an organizational assessment or employee survey.

There is also crossover in that a trend could be both an opportunity and a threat. For example, tax legislation changes could either be advantageous or disruptive depending on how the law is written.

We advocate for completing a SWOT both for the company and its competitors. This is useful because the strategies discovered can attempt to anticipate your company's future direction, or strategies of competitors. When completing a SWOT analysis, it may be useful for a management team to put themselves in their competitors' shoes.

CORE COMPETENCIES

The very term "core competency" is often misunderstood. The core competencies of a company reflect the range of capabilities, technologies and knowledge that directly deliver value to customers.

Core competencies are the source of economic value. Core competencies represent the attributes that the company's brand should be known for. These would also represent the activities that the company would insource (and never outsource) because they are central and integral to the brand promise.

Examples of core competencies could include:

- Production
- Sales and Marketing
- Design and Engineering
- Technology
- Access to materials, resources, markets or distribution

Our firm worked with a small manufacturing company that was having difficulty maintaining relevancy in the marketplace. The pace of technology change was such that the company could not employ enough engineers to develop a proprietary set of products.

However, the company had great relationships with customers and integrators. It was perceived as a market leader in part because of a mature sales organization. The company had excellent integration of marketing and sales. Recognizing its limitations, the company pivoted and focused on what it did best: sales and marketing.

It outsourced most of the production except for final assembly, so it could maintain control of quality. It hired contract engineers, realizing that even though it probably couldn't be first to market, it could develop technologies that were just good enough. An understanding of its true core competencies likely saved the company from financial ruin, and preserved jobs.

The moral of the story is that small and mid-market companies with limited resources cannot be good at everything. Gaining clarity about where to focus resources is a critical decision in a strategic plan.

UNIQUE SELLING PROPOSITION

"Unique selling proposition" and "value proposition" are used interchangeably. All suppliers must either identify as a low-cost leader or through a differentiated offer.

See Chapter 4 for methods on creating a unique selling proposition. The value proposition should be based on a set of guiding principles for how a provider demonstrates value.

Tools that can be used to create a value proposition:

– B2B Value Pyramid (Chapter 3)

– Value Fitness Test (Chapter 7)

A model that is useful in creating a unique selling proposition is to complete the following sentence:

To _____ (whom), our company is the _____ (point of differentiation) that provides _____ (point of differentiation) because _____ (reasons to believe).

CHANNELS OF DISTRIBUTION

Channels denote the systems or intermediates used for a product or service to reach its end user.[49] Naturally, channels vary greatly by products and services and from business to business. Each channel is worthy of its own strategy, and companies should regularly consider each as a new opportunity. Examples of channels may include:

- Distributor/Wholesaler/Partner
- Dealer
- Sales Direct
- Self-Distribution
- Sales Hybrid
- Web (self-serve)

TARGETS AND VERTICALS

Targets and verticals may be components of the Market Analysis or a standalone section within the strategic plan. One of the most critical elements of a growth plan is specific targeting of market and customers.

Marketers could be described as:

Mass: When selling to the "mass market," the supplier does not segment customers by type or need. Messaging is designed for a broad audience. Cell phone companies sell to the mass market.

Niche: Niche suppliers address a very specific market, which could be vertical or horizontal. A company offering heating and air conditioning only in Tampa would be considered a niche provider. Niche providers participate in few steps in the value chain.

Many companies serve only one or two vertical markets. For those that serve multiple verticals, an analysis of each vertical is warranted.

ITEMS TO INCLUDE IN YOUR ANALYSIS:

Top customers in the vertical
Percentage of revenue in the vertical
Percentage of total revenue
Percentage of vertical to total revenue

Retailer	U.S. Rank	Sales Rank	Record Year	Sales	CY Increase
Kroger	1	1	$421,134	$421,134	5%
Albertsons	2	2	$500,234	$420,584	-8%
Publix	3	3	$300,348	$300,348	2%
Meijer	8	4	$290,467	$290,467	1%
H-E-B	5	5	$165,261	$163,456	3%
Trader Joe's	10	6	$104,264	$104,264	5%
Delhaize	7	7	$91,035	$91,035	-10%
Ahold	4	8	$86,258	$86,258	0%

Grocery Channel: 24% of revenue
Channel Growth: 7%
Industry Growth: 3%

Then, compare the projected growth rates of industry verticals with the growth rate for the firm.

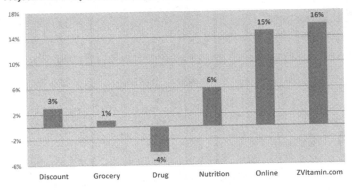

Projected Industry Growth Rate by Channel

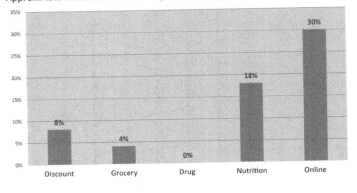

Approximate Incremental Growth by Domestic Market

> *I have found it counterintuitive that a more finite market promotes growth. Salespeople often believe any target is a good target.*

In fact, some companies enter a new market space by accident. Salespeople identify opportunities with customers, and sometimes these opportunities require activities outside the company's core competency. Management stretches itself to satisfy a customer or new prospect. In trying to fulfill the requirements, they realize they don't have the people, processes or technology to manage the business well. Without enough scale in the category, they lose money.

Entering any market should require a business plan (a scaled-down version of a strategic plan, with similar components as included in this section). Entry into any market should be supported by data.

- What is the size of the market?
- How fast is it growing?
- What competitors are already rooted in the space?

There is also a test that can be used for individual customers. Companies can create a scoring system to evaluate whether a potential customer fits their profile (see the Value Fitness Test in Chapter 7).

COST STRUCTURE

During the early stages of the Industrial Revolution, companies employed a cost-plus method to determine pricing. Today, many customers demand a certain price point, and providers must work backward to sell their goods and services accordingly.

Management teams must be highly intentional about establishing a cost structure to sell their goods and services at the right price point.

Cost structure examples include:

- **Cost Focus:** Keep costs low regardless
- **Growth Focus:** Investing in resources that support growth

- **Variable:** Costs that can scale with a business
- **Fixed:** Deploying capital at a fixed cost
- **Shared:** Costs that might be co-oped with others

MONETIZATION AND PRICING

Our experience has been that companies do not spend much time thinking about innovative monetization methods. Changing a pricing model is perhaps the quickest and easiest way to disrupt an industry with little investment.

Pricing (monetization) models include:

Usage-based: Rolls-Royce charges airlines for the usage of its engines. This approach is gaining steam as companies must fully utilize their assets.

Fee-for-service: Made popular by attorneys and CPAs, fee-for-service is the method used when professionals charge by the hour.

Distribution/Fee-for-product: Used when a distributor/agent charges a fixed cost.

Distribution/Activity-based costing: When a distributor charges based on actual cost depending on volume (for example, size of an order and quantity).

Fixed price: Used in project-based businesses to remove doubt on the part of a buyer.

Promotional/Advertising fees: Often used in franchising when a provider co-ops marketing or advertising and takes a markup.

Network or Platform: When a provider supplies end-to-end services and has many profit centers, including the sale of data.

Subscription: Often used in SaaS, when the provider charges a monthly fee and earns passive income.

Licensing: Provides permission for others to use your intellectual property.

Leasing: Providing access to assets owned by others.

Upsell: Using loss leaders to upsell high-volume merchandise.

Market/Real time: Financial arbitrage based on changing market conditions.

Suite of services: The classic "good/better/best" model. When providing three choices, most buyers will select the middle one.

Volume pricing: Based on buying mass quantities.

> *While all of these methods are valid, there is clearly movement in the economy toward subscription and pricing models that promote customers paying based on their actual usage.*

For example, software companies have moved to "software as a service" in an effort to bundle services and extract higher fees (as we cited earlier with Microsoft 365).

Ridesharing services provide a great example of consumers only paying for assets at the time they are consumed. This will continue to be a hot trend, as asset utilization is a key element to eliminating cost within our economy.

GO-TO-MARKET STRATEGY

The term "go-to-market strategy" generally encompasses the concepts covered in Chapter 7.

They include:
- Target Market
- Value Proposition
- Market Segmentation
- Competitive Analysis
- Distribution Channels
- Sales Strategy
- Marketing Plan/Branding

BRAND PROMISE

As with other topics in this section, branding is a broad topic that inspires many books. As a component of strategic planning, branding could be defined as the statement you make to customers that identifies what they should expect for all interactions with your people, products, services and company.

It is typical for mid-market companies (especially B2B) to have a small marketing department. When that is the case, the marketing department will typically take on the role of marketing services and focus on advertising, trade show booth coordination, sales materials, website and social media activities. Defining value proposition is often outside their purview.

Thus, there is confusion about such terms as *marketing strategy* and *branding*. As the name implies, brand promise is the set of characteristics customers can expect from the brand every time. Famously, FedEx reframed its industry with "When it absolutely, positively has to be there overnight."[50] Generally, a brand promise is less explicit and not stated as a guarantee.

A practical method for developing a brand promise is to establish a set of "pillars." These are the inherent characteristics of the brand. Famously, McDonald's has built its business on a promise that the food will be the same in every restaurant, it will be delivered quickly, and the bathrooms will be clean.

RESOURCES: PEOPLE, PROCESSES AND TECHNOLOGY

As a management team evaluates its strategy, it must weigh its existing resources and ability to execute. We typically define infrastructure as having three components: people, processes and technology.

PEOPLE

There are two specific elements of a human capital strategy that should be included in a forward-looking strategic plan:

Staffing Plan. How many people will need to be hired in the next three years? For example, in a manufacturing environment it may be:

Year 1
    10 factory workers (direct)
    3 supervisors (indirect)
    1 Director of Quality
    1 Vice President of Human Resources

A consideration in the staffing plan should be maintaining labor as a percentage of revenue that is at par or lower than past years.

Succession Plan. Who will be developed as future leaders of the organization?

Download our Succession Planning template at: *www.optimizeinc.net/downloads*

PROCESSES

Management should consider what tribal knowledge has been institutionalized. All core processes should be documented in written policies and procedures. For example, product development processes, which may be informal or undocumented, can be converted into a formal process, with flow charts that better institutionalize how decisions should be made, by when and by whom.

TECHNOLOGY

In some instances a company's technology is its product, and technology is considered in the value proposition and other sections of the strategic plan. In other cases, the usages of technology better represent tactics.

Management should think about what technology would enable better productivity in the future. Technology upgrades are often included in the capital planning process, which may occur in strategic planning or during the budgetary process.

VALUE DRIVER:
SCALABILITY AND SERVICE EXCELLENCE

Value Driver Tip—Business owners should ask of their teams: "How will technology be a competitive advantage for our company?"

For example, building a platform company generally requires costly and complex integrated systems. Too often, technology is viewed as a tool to make internal staff productive and is not outward focused. Ensure that technology has a seat at the table and that your strategic plan considers technology improvements to be made in the future.

FINANCIAL PROJECTIONS

One foundational element of a strategic plan consists of financial projections that demonstrate the company's momentum. It is useful to include at least one year of trailing data, as well as projections for the next three years. The following example references key elements that are often included in financial projections.

	2018	2019 Proj	2020 Proj	2021 Proj
Revenue	$40,000	$43,000	$47,000	$51,000
% Increase	8%	8%	9%	9%
GP	$16,000	$17,200	$18,330	$19,890
GP %	40%	40%	39%	39%
Sales and Marketing Expense	$3,200	$3,440	$3,760	$4,080
S&M %	8%	8%	8%	8%
General and Administrative	$8,800	$9,030	$9,400	$10,200
SG&A %	22%	21%	20%	20%
EBITDA	$4,000	$4,730	$5,170	$5,610
EBITDA %	10%	11%	11%	11%
% Growth	12%	18%	9%	9%

Download the financial projections guide here:
www.optimizeinc.net/downloads

EXECUTIVE SUMMARY

Although a strategy roadmap in summary form may not include an executive summary, a full strategic plan should include a brief narrative. An executive summary may be two to three pages presented first in the strategic planning document.

OBJECTIVES, GOALS AND ACTION ITEMS

In Chapter 11 we will provide a guide to goal setting. Generally, objectives, goals and action items provide the structure from which management can act and be held accountable.

There are multiple suitable structures for objectives, goals and action items. We typically employ a three-tier system that is either organized as:

Goal-Objective-Action, or
Objective-Goal-Action

As goals should be SMART, specifics about an outcome are typically listed in a goal and not an objective. For example:

> *Objective:* Expand East Coast Production Capacity
> *Goal:* Open facility with ability to produce 1,000,000 widgets by 2020
> *Action:* Hire construction consultant by 2/1
> *Action:* Hire architect by 4/1

Download an action plan template at:
www.optimizeinc.net/downloads

In our off-sites, we simplify the company's strategic plan and vision in the form of a two- to three-page strategy roadmap:

Download the template at:
www.optimizeinc.net/downloads

CHAPTER REVIEW

- ▶ Strategic planning should be a cycle and not an activity.
- ▶ A well-organized strategic planning cycle has a rhythm and cadence. The management team sets a long-term vision and a set of intermediate objectives and actions for the following year. They execute the plan. Then the

following year they repeat the process, moving long-term goals and objectives forward by a year.

▸ Perhaps counterintuitive to people who don't value them, the adoption of mission, values and vision statements can drive economic value.

▸ Salespeople often believe any target is a good target.

▸ There is clearly movement in the economy toward subscription and pricing models that promote customers paying based on their actual usage.

Strategic plan components include:

- Executive Summary
- Environmental Forces
- Market Analysis
- Strategy Roadmap
- Mission and Values
- Vision
- Strategic Objectives
- Financial Projections
- Action Plan

Tools Offered in this Chapter:

Strategy Roadmap
www.optimizeinc.net/downloads

Financial Projections Guide
www.optimizeinc.net/downloads

Action Plan Template
www.optimizeinc.net/downloads

Chapter 10
EXECUTION

"No strategic plan survives
its collision with reality."
—Unknown

FTER JAPAN BOMBED Pearl Harbor in 1941, President
Franklin Roosevelt addressed the nation. He said, "It
is not enough to turn out just a few more planes, a
few more tanks, a few more guns, a few more ships than can
be turned out by our enemies. We must out-produce them
overwhelmingly, so that there can be no question of our ability
to provide a crushing superiority of equipment in any theatre
of the world war."

America was not prepared for battle. In the years following the Great Depression, most Americans were reluctant
to engage in World War II. Just a few years earlier, the U.S.

had a cavalry of some fifty thousand, only the 39th largest in the world.[51]

President Roosevelt set forth aggressive goals for the nation: To produce 185,000 aircraft, 120,000 tanks and 55,000 anti-aircraft guns. He asked for Americans to contribute; he raised taxes, sold war bonds and imposed commodity rations.

In 1944, the U.S. produced more planes than Japan did in the entire war. By the end of World War II more than half of all of the world's industrial production occurred in the United States. Japan had the Imperial Japanese Navy Air Service. The United States had GM, Chrysler, Packard and the American people. The Japanese never had a chance.

The war turned because Americans understood why they needed to compete. President Roosevelt's goals aligned with a greater purpose, a mission that meant something to the people fighting the war.

In corporations, most employees complete their work on a daily basis, as instructed, without any idea of why their contributions are important.

I believe this is the reason for the notable lack of engagement on the part of the American workforce. The question of "what's in it for me" has not been answered for them. Employees need to know what and how much, but they also need to know why.

Gallup's annual Q12 Poll is the gold standard for measuring employee engagement. It includes the conclusions of 339 studies conducted across more than 82,000 companies and 1.9 million employees.[52] Gallup's Meta-Analysis compares financial performance of companies with high engagement to those with low engagement. Top quartile companies exceed bottom quartile companies in the following measures by the following amounts:

- Profitability—21%
- Sales productivity—20%
- Employee turnover—59%
- Absenteeism—41%
- In-patient safety incidents—58%
- Defects—40%

We have worked with great companies that tend to share some common attributes. They have a clear vision of the future. They communicate that vision and seek the engagement of their teams. They reinforce with visual management. They pursue the vision fanatically and measure the results.

In such companies, the routines and habits are embraced because they are accepted as the muscle that puts the company on the proper footing. Measurement is accepted, even celebrated, because it provides engaged employees with a pulse of the business. They not only want it; they need it.

My experience is that great strategy, when communicated well, improves results and drives greater engagement.

One of our clients is the City of Bend, Oregon. It employs over 500 people. Bend is a pretty eclectic place where quality of life and enjoying the great outdoors are a core part of the culture. Among its unique amenities, Bend built a kayak park on the Deschutes River, which runs through the center of town.

In conducting strategic planning for the City, I held more than a dozen focus groups where representatives from Bend's fire, police, administration and other departments came to share their opinions on the city's management and goals. As you might imagine, there are contentious issues within any city government. But the City of Bend takes time to listen and include employee feedback from the bottom up.

The City is highly regarded for its exceptional results in a series of metrics, including low use of force by its police department and low mortality rate for cardiac arrests (a function of response rate by fire/EMT). Many employees cite the City's strong communication as a reason for its success. So the execution of strategy has less to do with the strategies themselves and more to do with the organization creating them.

Execution is synonymous with discipline. To execute well requires that leaders create great habits within their organizations. Positive habits turn into muscles that make a team stronger. Great teams work together to flex their muscle and satisfy goals, as did the United States in World War II.

Earlier I referred to strategic planning and the discipline of execution that goes along with it—being more like a gym membership than a magic bullet. Just like a gym routine, muscle comes through hard work, focus and repetition. Strategic planning is a management ecosystem that binds together senior management and leaders throughout an organization.

Perhaps the biggest complaint we hear from management teams (the people executing strategy) is that when new initiatives are created, there are not new resources allocated to complete the work. We tend to pile on, not taking time to assess the workload of people taking on new projects. Often it is appropriate that an existing manager be tasked with handling a major initiative, but that should only occur after careful deliberation about their existing bandwidth.

Much of the time, a new objective or initiative is worthy of a dedicated project manager. For companies to be good at execution, they must build competency in project management. Project management is a skill that can be learned. Good project managers follow a disciplined approach in which they scope projects carefully, get input from constituents, communicate extremely well and manage expectations and milestones.

Companies of any size should have at least one person who is certified in project management (PMP—a professional designation offered by the Project Management Institute, or PMI), and who can be the champion of ad hoc projects. Others may require an entire project management team or department to manage projects in parallel. This approach aligns with our premise that those who are managing the core of a business cannot also be the innovators. The pressures of the day tend to win out over things that are new.

Although it may seem obvious that companies should have one central place where projects are managed, that is rarely the case. Companies can use software to manage projects, such as Microsoft Project or Basecamp. Or a simple action plan can be managed in a spreadsheet.

Simplified Action Plan by date: download at *www.optimizeinc.net/downloads*

Action Plan Example (ORGANIZED BY OBJECTIVE)

ZVitamin Action Plan 2018					
#	Action	Date	Champion	Assisted By	Notes
1	**Growth into New Segments**				
1A	Hire public relations consultant	3/1/18	Jill	Bob	
1B	Develop public relations plan and budget	4/1/18	Jill	Bob	
1C	Interview candidates for spokesman (M.D.)	5/1/18	Jill	Tom	
1D	Hire spokesman	6/15/18	Tom	Jill	
1E	Develop newsletter interface that can integrate with CRM	7/1/18	Phil	Karen	
1F	Hire salesman for pharmacy segment	7/15/18	Phil	Karen	
1G	Establish drip marketing plan	8/1/18	Jill		
2	**Outsourcing Volume Manufacturing**				
2A	Develop list of contract manufacturers through trade associations	Complete	Lisa		
2B	Develop vendor selection criteria	Complete	Lisa	Gary	
2C	Develop product specifications documentation	4/1/18	Jill	Amy	
2D	Develop process map	4/1/18	Jill	Amy	
2E	Complete initial interviews of potential partners	5/1/18	Tom	James	
2F	Complete onsite inspections	6/1/18	Tom		
2G	Develop partnership agreement	7/1/18	Tom	Kate	
3	**Expand Plant Capacity**				
3A	Develop lean budget	6/1/18	Angie		
3B	Hire lean expert	7/1/18	Angie		
3C	Develop lean best practices	10/1/18	TBD		
3D	Research 2nd shift options	11/1/18	TBD		
3E	Buy auto-rotate machine	11/1/18	Ted		
4	**Improve Cash Flow and Access to Capital**				
4A	Research new banking options (at lower rate)	11/30/18	Kate		
4B	Outsource product development at 10% savings	11/30/18	Gary	Rocket	
4C	Conduct pricing review of all B2C products	2/28/18	Kate		
4D	Conduct training of all managers on scheduling	6/1/18	Kate		
5	**Increase Average Transaction Via Custom Products**				
5A	Develop web content to support custom products	10/30/18	Rocket	Gary	
5B	Develop e-commerce custom features	11/30/18	Kate	Eric	

Some clients prefer to include red, yellow and green identifiers.

VALUE DRIVER:
PLANNING AND EXECUTION

Value Driver Tip—Here is a checklist of things companies should have in place to ensure excellent execution of strategy:

✓ Clear mission and vision that are clearly understood and unify staff

✓ Values that are ingrained in the culture of the company

✓ Clear mid-range SMART goals

✓ One-year objectives that prioritize how resources are to be deployed

✓ A dashboard or scorecard for the company, with metrics that employees understand

✓ Departmental goals and KPIs

✓ A strategic action plan with champions and dates, with specifics about who is going to do what

✓ A written strategic plan with all the points above

✓ Individual goals for every employee

✓ Monthly cross-functional meetings to review progress (versus strategic objectives) and to update the strategic action plan

✓ A decision tree or process for making key decisions on investments, projects and hiring people

✓ A parking lot of key issues that require attention in the future, but are not yet worthy of being listed on the existing action plan

✓ Regular meetings for management to gather feedback from employees

✓ A feedback loop rooted in values/behaviors and focused on performance

- ✓ A regular performance review process focused on employee contributions and closing the gap between employee self-ratings and employer ratings
- ✓ Thorough and updated job descriptions for every employee, learning plans and career paths
- ✓ A contemporary enterprise resource planning (ERP) level system supported by efficient workflows
- ✓ Policies and procedures documenting important work products

A trend that has been in vogue in recent years is agile development. Agile is spreading as a management system, going beyond its roots in development. Agile recognizes that teams cannot always anticipate or clearly define needs in advance, and that developers prefer to pivot based on real-time feedback of the code they have written.

As an overall management system, companies have a hard time making such a conversion. Managers have hard dates by which certain things need to be done. So, if you are implementing agile in your company, you still need a list of priorities and actions along with an understanding that they may need to shift regularly.

GUIDE TO GOAL SETTING

According to a recent poll in *Inc. Magazine*, only about 20 percent of business owners actively track business goals.[53] 23 percent of businesses achieve their business vision. One might wonder if these two numbers are correlated.

There is inherent value in tracking a business's progress against its strategic objectives, yet goal setting best practices have been debated, maligned and argued. The reality is that goal setting is part art and part science, and approaches differ from one management team to the next.

It is easy to get carried away with the science of developing numbers, which misses the point entirely. The art is engaging a team to take ownership of goals. That's why it is critical that a management team gathers input about the future and collaborates in the formation of goals. What's more, all departments need to have a voice in their creation. There is also artistry in how goals are articulated.

Below are answers to frequently asked questions about goal setting:

Why bother to set goals?

Goals can unify a team behind a common vision. Achieving goals can be quite exhilarating. Companywide goals can also set a foundation for the budget process and performance management.

What are SMART goals?

Although widely accepted as a standard for goal setting, the definition of the SMART acronym varies based on interpretation. One widely accepted definition is:

Specific
Measurable
Attainable
Relevant
Time Bound

The reason SMART has been so widely accepted (in addition to the clever play on words) is that many goals set by managers and employees are softballs. For example, a common soft goal is to "improve communication." While improving communication is highly relevant and achievable, this goal does not provide any specific measures that can be quantified over time. A SMART interpretation would be to "complete three communication training courses by March 1," or to "institute a monthly staff meeting with sales and engineering by June 15." These goals can be checked off a list as complete or quantified as above or below standard.

Should my goals be realistic or stretch?

The aggressiveness of an organization's goals is highly dependent on your answer to the first question—why are we setting goals in the first place? Some companies set aggressive growth targets that are the foundation for an incentive plan where growth is necessary and expected, and there is a need to stretch capabilities and people. Goals set for the purpose of setting a budget need to be highly realistic. For this reason, many companies set stretch goals to motivate people and lower targets as the foundation for budgets. Repeated failure to meet goals can be very demotivating, so it's important to set goals that are somewhat realistic.

What is the right time horizon? What is a BHAG?

The term BHAG stands for Big Hairy Audacious Goal, and was first made popular by James Collins and Jerry Porras in their bestselling book, *Built to Last: Successful Habits of*

Visionary Companies. A BHAG is the ultimate stretch goal, meant to unify a management team and organization around a hyper-aggressive, long-term goal. It often has a time frame of 10 years or more.

The current trend is to shorten time horizons to five years or less. It is important that goals be both aspirational and achievable.

What happens when my team fails to achieve our goals?

It is important to note the roadblocks to achieving a goal do not necessarily constitute failure. It may be that market conditions changed or that new resources will be necessary to achieve success. One of the reasons for setting goals is to bring focus to value drivers within a business. By measuring goals, you can bring additional focus to a problem or identify where additional resources may be needed.

The only time a goal should be recast is if there has been a shift in an uncontrollable external factor, such as an unexpected increase in raw material cost.

How do I know if my people are sandbagging?

Sandbagging is the art of purposefully underestimating performance. With new people, you can ask for justification of a goal based on some quantifiable proof. Managers are often fooled in this way. Fool me once, shame on you; fool me twice, shame on me. Don't let them get away with it the second time.

How do I get buy-in?

It is far more effective to have a team take part in setting a goal than it is to impose goals on them after the fact. It is important to get strong confirmation that a goal has been accepted and is not a subject of false agreement.

How does my company set financial goals if we do not practice open book management?

A common condition is an unwillingness of owners of private companies to share their business results with employees. Goal setting can provide an intermediate step, so employees can be held accountable without the need for sharing specific revenue or EBITDA (earnings before interest, taxes, depreciation and amortization) numbers. For example, a company could publicize the increase in revenue or profit as a percentage (Revenue YTD +7%), or focus on gross margin numbers.

WHAT ARE SOME OTHER TIPS TO MAKING GOALS MEANINGFUL?

- *Limit the number of goals to the vital few.* I recommend setting three to four main goals. There is an inverse relationship between the number of goals and the ability to implement them. The more goals, the harder it is.
- *Write them down and distribute the list.* It is common to set one group of goals for the management team and another list for wider distribution.

- *Create a system for reviewing your progress (scorecard).* It is critical to constantly score progress vs. goals.
- *Be patient.* Achieving goals takes time.

WHAT ARE SOME COMMON GOALS COMPANIES USE?

Goals should measure your strategic intent. While there are a multitude of options for setting goals, some commonly used goals are:

- Revenue
- Margin
- Labor
- EBITDA/Net profit
- Productivity/Utilization
- Growth in targeted business segments
- Revenue per employee
- Safety

Later in this chapter there is a list of key performance indicators that may be useful in goal setting.

WHAT IS THE DIFFERENCE BETWEEN A GOAL AND AN OBJECTIVE?

Although such terms are often interchangeable, goals are typically the quantifiable outcome of a broader objective. For example, a company may have an objective of diversifying into new markets, and a goal of growing by 20 percent in Europe.

Some organizations use the reverse and set a broad goal such as "Diversify our business by 20 percent" and a narrower objective of "Build a network of European distributors."

MANAGING CASH

There is another barrier to execution that every entrepreneur and management team must be keenly aware of. The number one threat to any new business is running out of cash.

It's counterintuitive to some that the more a company grows, the more pressure to generate cash flow. This is because a new business requires raw materials, labor and infrastructure that is not paid for yet. In other words, high-growth companies need more working capital than low-growth companies.

Although successful, stable companies are more bankable than smaller ones and can borrow at better rates, bank regulations and requirements can become onerous, tying a noose around a business.

VALUE DRIVER:
FINANCIAL HEALTH

Value Driver Tip—**All business owners
need to manage their cash cycle and be
aware of three things regarding their cash:
How much do they need? When will they
need it? Where will they get it?**

It is critical that a company manage its cash operating cycle. The cash operating cycle represents the time it takes to turn raw materials (or labor in the case of a service business) into cash. Think of a cash cycle as a continuum:

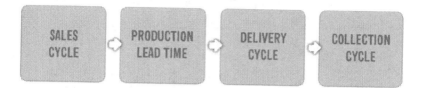

Many variables impact this cycle. For example, if a company has defects, that will push forward the operating cycle by thirty days or more. If freight takes seven days instead of five, the operating cycle expands. Management teams must actively manage the cycle to grow, or risk incurring higher carrying costs in the form of interest or required cash on hand.

A GUIDE TO CREATING STRATEGIC KEY PERFORMANCE INDICATORS (KPIs)

Another important variable in the execution of strategy is the ability to create meaningful scorecards. Scorecards (or dashboards) promote fact-based decision making. Companies that score well have a special energy, where employees understand why decisions they make directly contribute to the good of the company.

Our experience is that many companies are data rich and information poor. They have access to numbers but expect their managers and employees to hunt down the information (in the form of queries and the like). Departments tend to look at the numbers that affect them. Rarely are metrics pushed down to employees, and when they are, employees often don't understand why they are meaningful.

There are several important tenets of an effective scorecard methodology:

- Measurements must be strategically significant
- Measurements should be pushed (on some regular frequency) and not pulled
- The scorecard should be published as close to real time as possible (weekly is better than monthly)
- Numbers are in public view
- Employees are trained on what the numbers mean and why they are important

VALUE DRIVER:
TECHNOLOGY AND INFORMATION

Value Driver Tip—Growth companies develop meaningful KPIs that are published in public view, are understood by staff, and drive corporate performance.

As emphasized in The Balanced Scorecard methodology, made popular by authors Kaplan and Norton of Harvard Business School, many scorecards take on different "perspectives," such as:

- ***Emphasis on customers:*** Customer retention, customer satisfaction, customer service, business development, marketing, web and building new markets. Many companies look for this section to provide a snapshot of the sales pipeline and customer loyalty.

- *Emphasis on financial returns:* Quality of revenue, margins, receivables, inventory risk, and more. What are the variables that predict future profitability?
- *Emphasis on internal process:* Manufacturing, cycle time, technology, logistics, and so on. This section is inward-looking and focuses on operational excellence and efficiency.
- *Emphasis on learning and growth:* Development of human capital. This section focuses on development

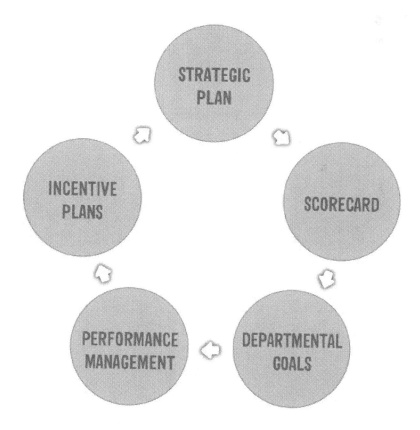

of people, team culture and activities that drive the performance of people.

Scorecards are a critical component within execution because they tie strategy to employee engagement and performance.

> *We often find that companies try to implement incentive plans that lack substance, because they are not tied to meaningful corporate measurements. A corporate scorecard should be the foundation on which departmental goals, performance management and incentive plans are built.*

The systems for measurement are different for every business, but as a rule, it's best not to use more than sixteen scorecard measures. Some numbers are conducive to weekly or even daily measurement, whereas others are more effectively measured monthly. Items that cannot be reported often (such as employee satisfaction) may not be appropriate on a scorecard.

Another consideration regarding what to measure revolves around what numbers can be easily tracked and reported. Many measures can be automated using an ERP or CRM, for example, whereas others require a lot of manual processing. Managers should evaluate the burden in gathering certain numbers and make a cost-benefit decision for each one.

In such instances, perfection might be overrated. It may be that a number is imperfect, but is 100 percent automated. To track such a metric could be more useful than one that requires a lot of number crunching. This is true as long as the result is apples to apples; if it is 80 percent accurate in April, it will be 80 percent accurate in May. There is often an argument that only perfect numbers should be used, especially if a scorecard is the basis for performance measures. Often, managers talk their way out of any objective measurement, which is less rational than using consistently imperfect numbers.

Here are some measures to consider:

CUSTOMER PERSPECTIVE

- Hourly, daily, weekly, monthly, quarterly and annual sales
- Revenue from new product categories
- Growth from new products
- Growth from new customers
- Market share
- Average order size
- Conversion rate
- Product performance (of key products)
- New customer orders vs. returning customer sales
- Cost of goods sold
- Product affinity (which products are purchased together)
- Inventory levels
- Competitive pricing
- Revenue per salesperson
- Pipeline: first meetings
- Pipeline: new contacts
- Pipeline: new opportunities

- Pipeline: new proposals submitted
- Pipeline: close ratio
- Pipeline: new clients added
- Sales by contact method
- Sales by channel
- CRM compliance
- Return on marketing investment
- Marketing impressions
- Number of marketing events (newsletters, white papers, webinars, testimonials)
- Incremental sales
- Web traffic
- Click-through rate (web)
- Search impressions
- Cost per new prospect/lead
- Site traffic
- Unique visitors vs. returning visitors
- Time on website
- Page views per visit
- Traffic source
- Time of day monitoring (when site visitors come)
- Newsletter subscribers (opt-in)
- Texting subscribers
- Chat sessions initiated
- Facebook, Twitter, or Internet followers or fans
- Pay-per-click traffic volume
- Blog traffic
- Number and quality of product reviews
- Brand or display advertising click-through rates

- Affiliate performance rates
- Conversion from prospect to client
- SEO keyword ranking
- Search results
- Subscribes to an RSS feed
- Call-to-action downloads
- Cost per lead
- Stickiness (pages/time viewed)
- Customer service email count
- Customer service phone call count
- Customer service chat count
- Average resolution time
- Complaints
- Concern classification
- Number of customer surveys completed
- Average customer retention
- First call resolution rate
- New customer retention rate
- Value of new business
- Net promoter score
- Average transaction
- Up-sales

FINANCIAL PERSPECTIVE
- Gross profit
- Profit growth
- Cost reduction
- Inventory turnover
- Return on equity

- Accounts receivable dollars
- Accounts receivable days
- Accounts receivable past 60/90 days
- Accounts receivable write-offs
- Working capital
- Percentage of invoices overdue when paid
- Return on capital employed
- Cash flow
- Invoice match rate
- Billing errors
- Date of closing
- Date of reporting
- Debt
- Credit line balance
- Internal service level (accounting)

INTERNAL PROCESS (MANUFACTURING, SUPPLY CHAIN, IT)

- Cycle time
- Utilization
- Rejection rate
- In-stock rate
- On-time delivery
- Inventory turnover
- Fill rate
- Accuracy rate (perfect order rate)
- Rejects
- Rework
- Backorder percent

- Out of stocks
- Inventory as a percentage of revenue
- Total production cost per unit
- Carrying costs of inventory
- Capacity
- Manufacturing schedule adherence
- Percentage of deliveries made on time
- Percentage of deliveries received on time
- Number of deliveries involving incorrect quantities
- Reduction in purchasing cost against quoted cost
- Cost of goods sold
- Work-in-process value
- Defects
- Scrap
- Fill rate
- IT costs as a percentage of revenue
- Uptime
- Number of new open tickets
- Response time on initial requests
- R&D as a percentage of sales
- Number of resolved tickets
- Mean time between failure (IT)
- Mean time to repair (IT)
- Internal service level operations
- Internal service level

LEARNING AND GROWTH

- Labor costs
- Retention

- Turnover rate
- Average length of staff retention
- Number of applications to vacancies advertised
- Successors named
- Corporate social responsibility
- Internal satisfaction rating
- HR tools implemented
- Reviews completed
- Recruiting cost per employee
- Percentage of new hires with 24 months service
- Percentage of managers receiving leadership training
- Training hours per employee
- Learning management system utilization
- Lost-time accidents
- Percentage of employees at competency level
- Average overtime hours
- Cost rate of total benefits
- Average income per employee hour
- Training cost per employee
- Accidents
- Ex-Mod (experience modification) rate
- Number of employees
- Number of hires
- New innovations generated
- R&D expense as a percentage of revenue

EFFECTIVE ORGANIZATIONAL STRUCTURES

Another barrier to execution is poor organizational design. An organizational structure is a hierarchy of people and functions.

> 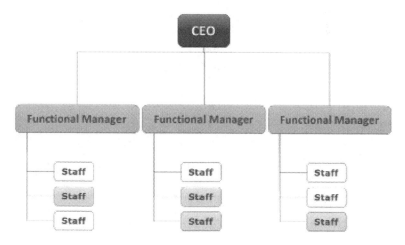 At maturity, contemporary organizations adopt one of the following three structure types:
> - *Functional structure*
> - *Divisional structure*
> - *Matrix structure*

Functional Structure

This structure is often found in operationally excellent companies that produce high volume at low cost. Functional structures promote specialization and standardization within the enterprise. Such standards ensure consistency and work quality.

The tradeoff in functional structures is that businesses and brands can lose their identity. Functional departments are less likely to conform to the individual needs of customers.

Such command and control methodologies can easily become bureaucratic. It is common for the interests of "functional departments" such as Accounting or IT to conflict with each other, promoting turf wars within the enterprise.

Divisional Structure

In a divisional structure each division is self-contained, manages its own resources and manages a separate P&L (profit and loss). Divisional structures are often deployed in companies with expansive geographic businesses (global brands). Divisional structures are more nimble and promote greater customer intimacy. Coordination and communication between departments can be constrained by organizational boundaries.

This structure also promotes duplicity of effort (multiple people in the same role) and higher costs. Within this structure, specialists report to generalists; for example, a Controller may report to a GM who does not know accounting. Such structures may create unhealthy rivalry across divisions.

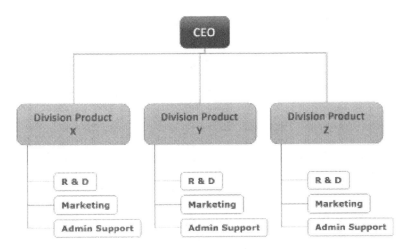

Matrix Organization

A matrix organization is a hybrid that blends the best attributes of functional and divisional structures. A matrix endorses identity for brands and products, but supports them through centralized administration. Over the last twenty years, matrix organizations have gained popularity in multinational enterprises.

Matrix organizations can be complex and frustrating. For a matrix organization to thrive, a work culture that supports "cross-functional" teams is required. For example, if a company's IT infrastructure were to support multiple divisions, there would need to be consensus on each division's technology needs. Each division would have to give up its ability to directly manage its own IT resources. The dual management approach found in a matrix organization may be the most difficult for senior leadership to manage, so clarity around roles and responsibilities is critical. For example, there are more "dotted line" relationships in a matrix organization, which

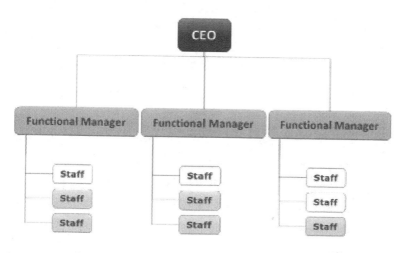

can cause triangulation and confusion. Managers within a matrix organization must be willing to share authority with counterparts from divisions and functions.

CHAPTER REVIEW

- ▸ Growth companies develop meaningful KPIs that are published in public view, are understood by staff and drive corporate performance.

- ▸ Companies may try to implement incentive plans that lack substance because they are not tied to meaningful corporate measurements. A corporate scorecard should be the foundation on which departmental goal setting, performance management and incentive plans are built.

- ▸ At maturity, contemporary organizations adopt one of the following structure types:
  - ○ Functional structure
  - ○ Divisional structure
  - ○ Matrix structure

Other keys to execution include:

- ▸ Clear mission and vision that are understood and unify staff
- ▸ Values that are ingrained in the culture of the company
- ▸ Clear midrange SMART goals

- One-year objectives that prioritize how resources are to be deployed

- Departmental goals and KPIs

- A strategic action plan with champions and dates, with specifics about who will do what

- A written strategic plan with all the points above

- Individual goals for every employee

- Regular (monthly) cross-functional meetings to review progress against strategic objectives, and to update the strategic action plan

- A decision tree or process for making key decisions on investments, projects and hiring people

- A parking lot of key issues that require attention in the future, but are not worthy of being listed on the existing action plan

- Regular meetings for management to gather feedback from employees

- A feedback loop rooted in values/behaviors and focused on performance

- A regular performance review process focused on employee contributions and closing the gap between employee self-ratings and employer ratings

- Every employee has a job description, learning plan and career path

- ► A contemporary enterprise resource planning (ERP) level system supported by efficient workflows
- ► Policies and procedures documenting important work products

Tools Offered in this Chapter:

Action Plan Template
www.optimizeinc.net/downloads

Chapter 11
PREPARING FOR AN EXIT

"It's far better to buy a wonderful company at a fair
price than a fair company at a wonderful price."
—Warren Buffett

ENTREPRENEURS HAVE DIFFERENT motivations for
building their businesses. Some are adrenaline junk-
ies who get satisfaction from creating something from
scratch. Others invest for more altruistic reasons. But most I
have worked with aspire to participate in a transaction (sale).

Because of shifting demographics and the aging U.S.
population, more entrepreneurs will seek retirement in the next
10 years than at any other time in history. It is estimated that
baby boomers own 12 million U.S. businesses, representing
$10 trillion in assets, and that 70 percent of those companies
will be sold in the next 15 years.[54] This would provide for an
unparalleled M&A market for private companies.

We have found that entrepreneurs can fall into a trap; they fantasize their entire life about a liquidity event (selling their business), believing that their life's work will be validated upon a sale. Yet the grass is not always greener on the other side. Most of them know they cannot realize a return on capital outside the business that remotely resembles the cash flow generated by a mid-market company. Plus, they need to find something to do.

I always like to point out that divesture is only one method of raising cash. In some instances, it may be advantageous for entrepreneurs to "take chips off the table" with a recapitalization, which often takes on the form of selling a minority stake in their business.

Companies can also borrow money to expand, providing the business owner with a respite from funding the business. In other cases, an entrepreneur may be better off keeping a business and putting an experienced CEO (hired gun) into place, reaping excess cash flow into their retirement.

When the risks of running the business are far greater than keeping it, they should consider an exit strategy. That is, if cash flow is rapidly increasing, the math may favor keeping the business. If risk is moderate, the business owner may consider a recap (recapitalization).

> *It is common for business owners to sell a business and then feel devalued once they are no longer needed to make all the decisions. After a transaction, it is critical that business owners find a new purpose.*

We are purposeful about preparing business owners for such events, and have deliberate conversations about their exits. There are several important considerations for business owners, which they should be planning for at least three to five years before a transaction:

- Have they achieved relevance in the business to the extent that they can affect a high-value transaction?
- Have they carefully considered the attributes that will be important to a buyer (depth of the management team, unique value proposition, scalable systems, and so forth)?
- Have they benchmarked the business to understand its relative value when compared to similar businesses?
- Has the owner considered the tax implications of a transaction to minimize their exposure?
- Have all the succession/estate plan elements been formalized?
- Have they ensured that key talent is "handcuffed"?

We have found that business owners think a lot about the "transaction" and not about the activities that must be completed pre- and post-transaction. For example, the creation of an ESOP (employee stock ownership plan) can eliminate much of an owner's tax liability. It is estimated that less than 20 percent of business owners have a formal, written exit plan.[55]

For this reason, business owners need to enter a value acceleration phase to ensure that certain pre-sale conditions are met. This may include activities such as pivoting to audited financial statements or other actions that could mitigate risk for a buyer.

M&A (mergers and acquisitions) are complex, costly and not for the faint of heart. The process is extremely time consuming and fraught with risk. Yet such divestures can provide shareholders and management teams with a payoff for their life's work.

Naturally, M&A is a high-stakes endeavor. Buyers, who are usually more seasoned than sellers, will try to take advantage of a seller's inexperience and attempt to knock her off her perch with a dizzying array of challenges to her assumptions, financial statements, operations, and more. Buyers are adept at gaining leverage and discounting price. Sellers should be prepared for this form of warfare and *must* be surrounded by the right advisors who can navigate the terrain.

The expected increase in the volume of transactions will shape a market with greater supply, making such routines even more critical. Throughout this work, we have offered "value drivers"—important factors in driving enterprise value. These are the drivers a management team should focus on whether they are growing a business to keep it or growing a business to sell it. They are the same factors buyers use in their evaluation of a business.

To repeat, the value drivers are:

1. Unique value proposition and branding that proves value
2. Diversified markets and customers
3. Business model and sustainable revenue model
4. Financial health
5. Sales competency and customer relationships
6. Right people in the right seats
7. Leadership and culture
8. Technology and information
9. Scalability and service excellence
10. Planning and execution

To download our Exit Planning white paper, go to: *www.optimizeinc.net/exit-planning*

Collectively, these value drivers improve a buyer's ability to predict future performance, much like they improve the probability of success in any business. Most importantly, buyers want to ensure a target company's revenue and profitability are sustainable. Generally, buyers assume about a 20 to 30 percent loss in the customer base during a transaction. The management team's ability to convince buyers of the business's stability ratchets up or down such assumptions.

Even modest improvements in business performance can drive disproportionate increases in value, because of the value multiplier effect.

Consider the following chart:

Scenario	A	B	C	D	E
Revenue	$25.0M	$30.0M	$30.0M	$35.0M	$35.0M
EBITDA	$2.5M	$3.00M	$3.5M	$4.2M	$4.6M
EBITDA %	10%	10%	12%	12%	13%
Multiple	5.0	5.0	5.5	5.5	6.0
Enterprise Value	$12.5M	$15M	$19.3M	$23.1M	$27.3M

Assume the company's current state is scenario A, $25 million in revenue at 10% EBITDA. Further assume the management team was successful and:

- Grew the business from $25 million to $35 million
- Moved the EBITDA margin from 10 percent to 13 percent

Now that the company has cleared the $5 million EBITDA threshold, it is more likely to court private equity suitors, driving up the multiple. So assuming a multiple of six instead of five (one turn in industry parlance), with only slightly higher revenue and EBITDA, the improvement delivers a whopping 118 percent increase in enterprise value.

> *In my experience, the biggest mistake an entrepreneur can make in preparing for an exit is to lose patience in the process.*

Oftentimes there are peaks and valleys during the cycle, causing business owners to panic, which can lead them to sell before they have optimized value. I refer to those who wait for their companies to reach the tipping point of value as patient sellers.

Patient sellers ensure the following conditions are met before entering into the fray:

- Have minimized their concentration risk. Risk varies by industry, but a good rule is to have no industry vertical represent more than 40 percent of volume, no customer more than 15 percent, and have 80 percent of volume spread out over at least a dozen customers.
- Have a minimum of three years of consistent revenue and EBITDA growth of 7 percent or more. High-growth industries may require more momentum, and legacy businesses may require less.
- Have developed a growth story (as part of their strategic plan) that can pass the "smell test," demonstrating where future growth will come from. All claims must be supported by data and analysis. Buyers will vet every number.
- Flawless financial statements and reporting, with no unusual items on their balance sheet.

- Strong, stable margins. Declining margins are a clear warning sign that a business has not differentiated its offer.
- EBITDA margins exceeding industry benchmarks. Low margin businesses generate low multiples.
- They have a well-thought-out succession plan, populated with people who will not be leaving at the time of the owner's exit (ensuring the buyers continuity during and after the process).
- Have recruited and developed strong managers who can grow with the buyer.
- Have placed handcuffs on key staff in the form of "participation bonuses." Participation bonuses are not equity and thus do not muddy the water or dilute shares. They are incentives paid to management to stay on through a transaction. Such bonuses can be absorbed by a buyer.
- No material labor actions or lawsuits that could disrupt a deal or carry a burden after a close.
- Engaged with reputable advisors whose statements are believable.

At minimum, to sell a mid-market company, the seller needs representation from a qualified investment banker, transactional attorney, CPA and wealth advisor/exit planner. Selling a business requires a team.

Sellers often make the mistake of working with their existing bankers and attorneys, as opposed to M&A specialists who know their industry. There are strong dynamics at play in such markets, and knowing potential strategic buyers and financial/private equity firms is critical. You don't want to lose the marathon in the last hundred yards because you decided not to pay the right advisors. It is not unusual for an investment bank to earn a $1 million fee for a mid-market transaction, and the entire transaction cost could be as much as three to four percent of the sale price.

Traditionally, strategic buyers have paid a premium for a company's strategic value. Today, private equity firms are under tremendous pressure to deploy their capital.

This is why a good investment banker is worth his weight in gold. Other activities fulfilled by the banker include:

- Providing extensive due diligence on the market and company
- Clarifying buyer preferences, which will inform on how to position the business for sale
- Providing a "fair value" opinion
- Developing a financing structure and providing access to debt financing when needed
- Preparing teaser materials for distribution to a targeted list of buyers
- Collaboration with transactional attorneys to create a non-disclosure agreement (NDA) and other relevant documents
- Creating a password-protected "data room" where potential buyers can access information
- Preparing executives for management presentations

- Preparing a "pitch book"
- Reviewing "Indication of Interest" letters
- Facilitating management visits with targeted buyers
- Reviewing formalized letters of intent
- Negotiating on behalf of the seller
- Closing the transaction

Aggressive buyers will attempt to preempt the process through "exclusive" offers. Accepting such terms dissuades other bidders from spiking the value of bids. An exclusive offer dilutes the selling price and should be avoided, unless the seller's objective is a speedy close.

During the buying process, bankers weed out potential buyers based on their ability to pay through Indications of Interest (IOIs), management visits and final offers.

When a business is not generating an operating profit, its value will be determined from the value of its real assets. In some industries it is common to determine value based on revenue. But the most accepted method for valuation is a compilation of comparable market multiples and discounted cash flows.

> *A business's value is based on a multiple of what cash the business will generate after considering the net present value of money and discounts for macro-, industry- or company-specific risks.*

Private equity firms have a reputation for being brutish and demanding in how they treat the management of companies they acquire. They expect structure and precision in the portfolio businesses they operate and often appoint board members and senior executives to govern them. Thus, managers are often intimidated by private equity firms and need to be educated about their methods.

Entrepreneurs are sometimes unprepared for the toll a transaction can take on them and their team. Managers will be in the unique position of having to present in high-pressure meetings while also under the stress of potentially losing their jobs.

A divesture could take a year, and during that time key management staff may be distracted by having to satisfy the needs of bankers and buyers. In particular, the financial staff will be under constant duress. Many companies hire interim accounting and finance firms to provide additional bandwidth during this stage.

There is an important caveat relating to retention of management teams. Every situation is different, but financial buyers tend to keep management teams in place. In a bolt-on acquisition of a like business, some positions may be redundant and will be eliminated. It is the assumption of a buyer that they will be able to realize efficiencies and reduce cost.

Some business owners are skittish about including key employees in the preparatory stages of a transaction, out of fear that they may flee. While confidentially being compromised is a legitimate concern, it is nearly impossible to contain the transaction team's activities. Investment bankers and buyers need information on every facet of a business, and technical due diligence can be extreme. Business owners should be intentional about creating a circle of trusted managers who can serve on a transition team and are rewarded at its successful conclusion.

Retention bonuses usually have a clause voiding the incentive if the employee reveals the nature of the provision or the intention to sell. The provision can include partial payment by the selling entity, as well as guarantees for employment with additional payment by the purchasing entity (thus defraying part of the cost to the buyer).

Buyers will often attempt to negotiate an earn-out, where the seller takes part of their compensation in the form of a consulting contract, or deferral of payments. It is important to note the pitfalls of earn-outs. The seller is often enthused by the prospects of a smooth transition and the potential to earn additional income after the business is sold.

However, fewer than 50 percent of sellers realize the full earn-out. This is because they tend to hold onto old processes that the buyer tries to replace, or they interfere with new lines of authority. At some point the entrepreneur needs to let go. Sellers should avoid earn-outs (unless there are tax or other benefits when doing so) or at the very least, put clear provisions in place to protect their interests.

The challenges of selling a business cannot be understated. The risks for an unsuccessful transaction are high. Yet, a successful sale can offer the culmination of a lifetime of blood, sweat and tears and result in extraordinary wealth.

CHAPTER REVIEW

▸ It is common for business owners to sell a business and then feel devalued once they are no longer needed to make all the decisions. After a transaction, it is critical that business owners find a new purpose.

▸ The biggest mistake an entrepreneur can make in preparing for an exit is to lose patience in the process.

▸ Oftentimes there are peaks and valleys during the cycle causing business owners to panic, which leads them to sell before they have optimized value. I refer to those who wait for their companies to reach the tipping point of value as patient sellers.

▸ A business's value is based on a multiple of what cash the business will generate after considering the net present value of money and discounts for macro-, industry- or company-specific risks.

Value Drivers:

1. Unique value proposition and branding that proves value
2. Diversified markets and customers
3. Business model and sustainable revenue model
4. Financial health
5. Sales competency and customer relationships
6. Right people in the right seats
7. Leadership and culture
8. Technology and information

9. Scalability and service excellence
10. Planning and execution

Tools Offered in this Chapter:

Exit Planning White Paper
www.optimizeinc.net/exit-planning

Chapter 12
FINAL THOUGHTS—
LEAD WITH VISION

"The road to success is always under construction."
—Lily Tomlin

A S I MENTIONED EARLIER, my first book, *Intended Consequences*, reflects a personal philosophy that I have about the world. I believe we are all in control of our own life and legacy and should conduct ourselves with clear intention.

I've had the privilege and honor of working with over 100 entrepreneurial business owners. They gravitate to me and to our practice because they too are intentional people. They are the type of people who care more about the quality of their movements than the quantity. They are the people who have a clear vision of what they want from life.

Thus, they seem to get more out of it than others. Entrepreneurship affords business owners the freedom to experience life to the fullest. Entrepreneurs not only reap financial rewards, but they tend to create balance for themselves and their families. They meet extraordinary people and do extraordinary things.

There is reason to have a vision and lead with it; it's simply a better way to live. It is remarkably fulfilling to set a goal and see it through. It is fulfilling to create products or services the market values. It is even more satisfying to see employees become the best versions of themselves.

We have provided the tools for creating a business vision, but we must also make a distinction between creating a vision and leading with one. Leading with a vision means keeping that vision front and center as if it were a living, breathing organism.

VALUE DRIVER:
LEADERSHIP AND CULTURE
Value Driver Tip—Lead with Vision

I always pay attention to the visual cues (visual management) within an office or facility. What you see, including the reinforcement of mission, values and vision, tells you a lot about a company's leadership.

If there were a bell curve illustrating CEO performance, it is those who lead with vision that move from mere competence to the edge of the curve, mastering their craft. Malcolm Gladwell famously claimed that it takes ten thousand hours to be an expert at something. It may take ten thousand hours of reinforcement in mission, values and vision to build an extraordinary company.

While this is fundamentally a strategy book, I hope you have drawn some inspiration from it. I hope you are clear on your vision and purpose. It is hard to lead and inspire others unless you are inspired yourself. I have found that companies with complete clarity around their end game, objectives and measurements have better alignment and rhythm. Management teams that are intentional about their actions get better results than those running their business in an ad hoc manner.

It is often the same people who live a purpose-driven life who are also able to articulate their vision to others. Employees have pretty good bullshit meters and can see right through people who are not authentic in their motivations.

By definition, to be extraordinary means doing things beyond what is ordinary. The companies that squeeze the extra 10 percent out of their employees are the ones that reach a deep level of engagement with them. They attract the best talent. They outperform the rest because their people are fanatical about achieving something bigger than themselves. Therefore, leading with vision means making sure a group of people buy in to a set of principles and methods that separate their organization from the pack.

A well-articulated vision can inspire people to set aside their own egos and move as one. It is the few, not the many, who are able to build such bonds with their investors, employees and customers.

There is a scene in the movie *Miracle,* depicting Coach Herb Brooks' pre-game speech before the U.S. hockey team took the ice against the Soviet Union in the 1980 Olympic Games.

He addressed his team while they sat quietly in the locker room: "Great moments are born from great opportunity. That's what you've earned here tonight. One game. If we played 'em ten times they might win nine. But not this game, not tonight.

"Tonight we skate with them. Tonight we stay with them and we shut them down, because we can. Tonight we are the greatest hockey team in the world. You were born to be hockey players. You were meant to be here tonight. This is your time. Their time is done. It is over. I am sick and tired of hearing about what a great hockey team the Soviets have. This is your time; now go out there and take it."

The Americans grabbed their sticks and headed toward the ice. They entered the arena to deafening chants of "USA! USA! USA!" The rest was history. I still get goosebumps watching the scene—a depiction of the greatest sports memory of my life.

The Soviets were practically unbeatable. They had won six of the last seven gold medals and had embarrassed the Americans 10–3, days before the start of the games in Lake Placid. There is only one reason the U.S. beat the Soviets and won the 1980 Olympic Gold Medal. It is because they believed they could.

After the United States liquidity crisis and "Great Recession," many entrepreneurs experienced a crisis of confidence. Employees had been beaten down; their wages, benefits and opportunities had been slashed. Businesses stopped investing.

During the liquidity crisis and the giant sucking sound that followed, I worked with many entrepreneurs who had to rediscover their mojo. I have a vivid memory of sitting with an incredibly talented young CEO who teared up, unsure of what the future might bring. Her business was floundering and she feared she might not be able to sustain her position as an industry leader. She found the strength and fortitude to build her company up again, using some of the principles in this book. To be fair, it was not that I provided her some magical insight. She just had to find the strength to gut it out.

A critical factor in building a successful company is confidence. A management team must be confident that their products are worthy of the prices they charge. You have to believe.

It's your time. It is time to charge the hill. If you have salespeople who don't believe and are not ready to charge it with you, it's time to wish them luck in their next position, wherever that might be. If your operations people do not believe they can improve cycle time and quality, fire them and find people who do. That includes eliminating staff incapable of charging the hill because they do not align with your values or lack skill or fortitude. You owe it to the others within your company to surround yourself with people who can and will do battle with you.

From our unique standpoint as strategists, we have seen entrepreneurs and their key employees fulfill their dreams. Anything is possible when you put your mind to it. Clarity about purpose enables confidence.

Webster's defines momentum as "the impetus and driving force gained by the development of a process or course of events." To gain momentum requires bold action and many smaller intangible activities that drive a company forward.

But to achieve nirvana requires a unique mindset. The managers mired in mediocrity are often the ones who feel they have to be right. The innovative, best-in-class entrepreneur is more interested in considering a wide range of views. Anyone can be right when you consider a finite group of ideas. To consider a broad range of ideas requires the willingness to listen and to be wrong. It is humility that moves entrepreneurs from good to great.

This is why innovation is so hard. To innovate is an acknowledgment that the status quo is not good enough. We have made the business case that best-in-class companies of the future will provide end-to-end solutions. That will require an uncommon commitment to discipline and continuous improvement.

In our work, we have had the opportunity to witness the value that can be unleashed within organizations committed to achieving greatness. We have worked with uncommon organizations that:

- Supply critical parts to 40 percent of the world's pacemakers
- Provided the optics for the Navy Seals who killed Osama bin Laden

- Make retirement available to hardworking Americans
- Supply wheelchairs for children in need
- Educate children and expose them to new skills
- Calibrate critical blood tests that save lives
- Provide solutions to students refinancing their debt
- Manufacture vital parts for fighter jets and airplanes
- Make healthy options available to the public
- Work with the aging and weak to provide them with more options
- Make the best beer in the world
- Are devoted to reducing usage of water and precious resources
- Work to relieve their city's traffic and improve police and fire protection

This is just a sample of what is possible when groups of people share a common vision. I have no doubt that our way of thinking has made the world a better place.

Greatness is rare because most people do not have the will, patience and discipline to succeed. In the introduction to this book, I said there would be no shortcuts. Strategic planning and the other methods we have advocated for require methodical, painstaking work. It is not for the weary.

For me, being purpose-driven has meant providing a model to my children in terms of values and how I live. It has meant a lot of nonprofit board work and pro bono retreats for nonprofits in my community. It has also meant being vulnerable and being clear about my deficits. Being clear about your strengths and weaknesses is the only way to improve.

So what should you do after reading this book? I hope you will apply the principles by:

- Sharing your strategic plan with key external stakeholders, like a board of directors, board of advisors or peer group.

- Sharing your strategic plan with key internal stakeholders, including key employees. You should share the broader vision with the entire company in a thoughtful way.

- Putting your plan in action by ensuring your management team meets monthly to review progress on your objectives and action items.

- Building a system to review your KPIs regularly.

- Rinsing and repeating your strategic planning process regularly.

- Making damn sure that you are the best employer in your space, including providing opportunities for your employees to learn and prosper.

Success is a dangerous tonic. It can lull people into a belief that they have things figured out. It is easy to become complacent. We have all seen those people who seem to have it all- success, happiness, health and families who love them. They tend to be the same people with a plan. They are the ones who know exactly what they want and how to get it.

I hope you find and keep your momentum. In your business and in your life, people will pay attention to how you show up. So, have the humility to prepare. Let's all make Vin Scully proud.

CHAPTER REVIEW

▸ It is those who lead with vision who move from mere competence to the edge of the curve, mastering their craft.

▸ It may take ten thousand hours of reinforcement in mission, values and vision to build an extraordinary company.

MARC EMMER is an author, speaker and consultant recognized as a thought leader throughout North America as an expert in strategy and strategic planning.

Marc founded Optimize Inc., a California-based consulting firm in 2002. Optimize has an impressive client list that includes public companies such as CBRE, Justice Stores (formerly Limited Too), Superior International and mid-market companies in a diverse range of industries including financial services, healthcare, technology and energy. Marc has personally facilitated strategy sessions for over 135 companies.

Marc is an accomplished speaker, having delivered over 275 keynote speeches for organizations such as Starbucks, Panda Express, the Association for Corporate Growth, and The Professional Coaches and Mentors Association, and speaks internationally for Vistage, the world's largest CEO peer group organization. His strategy blog is received by over a thousand senior executives.

In 2015, he was nominated in his community of Santa Clarita for Man of the Year to recognize his non-profit service. Marc's firm is active in its community, supporting The American Cancer Society, The Arthritis Foundation, The Boys and Girls Clubs of America, Soroptimist International, and many others. Marc has served on numerous for-profit and non-profit boards and is past Board Chairman of the SCV School and Business Alliance and Single Mothers Outreach. In order to provide non-profit leadership, Marc completed the rigorous non-profit training offered by the Annenberg Foundation at USC (by invitation only).

Reach Marc at marc@optimizeinc.net
For bookings, contact info@optimizeinc.net
For book orders of 10 or more contact
info@optimizeinc.net
Individual copies available on Amazon

www.optimizeinc.net

REFERENCES

[1] "The Mighty Middle," The Economist, October 2012

[2] SUSB Annual Data Tables—United States Census Bureau

[3] "Avoid the Traps that Can Destroy Family Businesses" by Stalk and Foley, Harvard Business Review, February 2012

[4] "Celebrating 10 years of GPS for the masses" by Dong Ngo, CNET

[5] Association for Corporate Growth

[6] Adapted from *The Innovator's Dilemma* by Clayton Christensen, HarperBusiness 2011

[7] Differing Competencies: as seen on Ted by Knut Haanaes, Boston Consulting Group

[8] "Bursting the CEO Bubble" by Hal Gregersen, Harvard Business Review (with quotes from Donald Rumsfeld)

[9] *Edge Strategy* by Alan Lewis and Dan McKone, Harvard Business Review Press

[10] *Five Frogs on a Log* by Feldman and Spratt—PricewaterhouseCoopers

[11] Special Year End Edition Oil Patch Bankruptcy Monitor, Haynes and Boone

[12] "90 Percent of All Purchasing Decisions Are Made Subconsciously," ISPO News

13 "Korean culture may offer clues in Asiana Crash," Heesun Wee, CNBC

14 "Asiana Pilot Was 'Very Concerned' About Landing at SFO Before Crash" by Dan Brekke, KQED News

15 *The Innovator's Method* by Nathan Furr and Jeff Dyer, Harvard Business Review Press

16 "Bursting the CEO Bubble" by Hal Gregersen, Harvard Business Review (with quotes from Donald Rumsfeld)

17 The Global Innovation 1000 Strategy

18 *Understanding Michael Porter* by Joan Magretta, Harvard Business Review Press

19 *Understanding Michael Porter* by Joan Magretta, Harvard Business Review Press

20 *The Three-Box Solution* by Vijay Govindarajan, Harvard Business Review Press

21 "10 New Uses for Old Inventions" by William Harris, *HowStuffWorks*

22 *Different* by Youngme Moon, Crown Press

23 "Under Armour," Wikipedia

24 "Blockbuster CEO once passed up a chance to buy Netflix for only $50 Million" by Celena Chong, Tech Insider

25 Distribution of movie and TV Rental Market, Statista

26 GIL Abu Dhabi Mega Trends by Frost & Sullivan

27 "Megatrends 2020" by Peter Diekmeyer, Zero Hedge

28 *The Industries of the Future* by Alec Ross

29 *The Industries of the Future* by Alec Ross

30 Marketsandmarkets.com

31 *The Industries of the Future* by Alec Ross

32 *The Industries of the Future* by Alec Ross

33 *The Industries of the Future* by Alec Ross

34 *The Industries of the Future* by Alec Ross

35 "The 4 Trends That Will Change the Way We Work," Upwork

36 "Freelancers Make Up 34 Percent of the U.S. Workforce" by Martin Konrad, Entrepreneur [https://www.entrepreneur.com/article/275362]

37 "10 Tips for Mastering an On-Demand Labor Model" by Scott Lancet, Worksmart

38 Employers in the On-Demand Economy, National Employment Law Project

39 "Building a digital banking-business" by Barquin and HV, McKinsey Financial Services

40 *The Challenger Sale* by Matthew Dixon and Brent Adamson

41 Civilian labor force participation rates, The Bureau of Labor Statistics

42 NLS New Release—The Bureau of Labor Statistics

43 Employee Financial Wellness Survey, PricewaterhouseCoopers

44 "Employee Turnover Costs and the Importance of the First Year," Celayix Software

45 "Seven minutes a day: the modern-day excuse for a parent" by Clifton Chadwick, The National Opinion

46 "CDC study finds America has never been more obese" by Zach Epstein, BRG

47 "Insufficient Sleep Is a Public Health Problem," Centers for Disease Control

48 "Keeping it in the Family" by Lewis Braham, Bloomberg Businessweek

49 Michael Porter's "Five Forces"

50 Porter's five forces analysis," Wikipedia

51 War Production, PBS

52 Gallup's Q12 Meta-analysis

53 Gallup's Q12 Meta-analysis

54 "Baby Boomers: Incredible Numbers are Buying and Selling Businesses," CA Business Brokers Association

55 Exit Planning Institute

INDEX

Made in the USA
San Bernardino, CA
16 March 2018